I0792995

CROOKED POLITICS in NORTHWEST INDIANA

JERRY DAVICH

THE History PRESS

Published by The History Press
Charleston, SC
www.historypress.net

First published 2017

Manufactured in the United States

ISBN 978.1.46713.642.6

Library of Congress Control Number: 2016956921

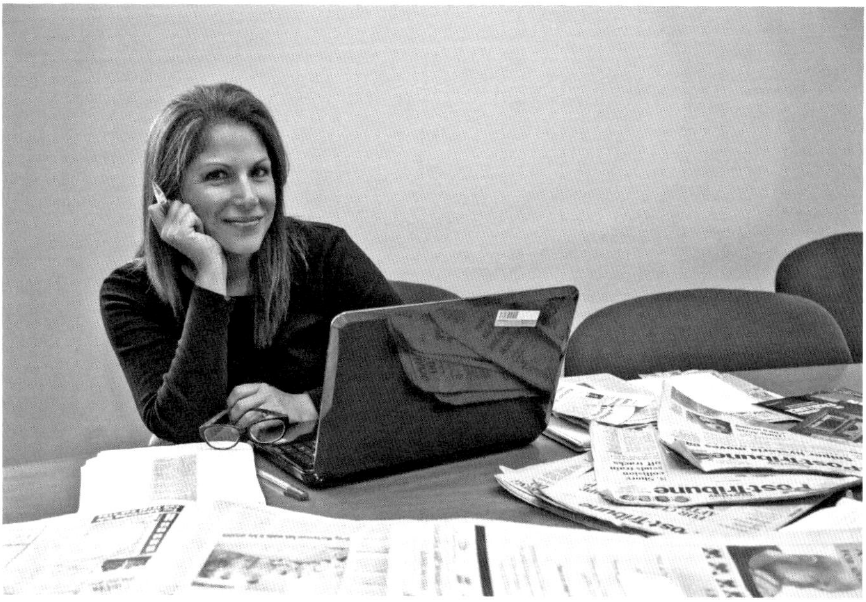

Karen Walker Davich. *Courtesy of Joey Lax-Salinas.*

To Karen, who not only helped research the findings and key passages within these pages but who also gave birth to the notion of writing it in the first place. This book would not have seen the light of day if not for her labor, passion and perseverance. Together, we view this book as our second child, following the 2015 birth of Lost Gary, Indiana, *our first published offspring.*

Contents

Contents

Foreword

Prior to my appointment to the police department, I was probably among the most politically naïve people in East Chicago.

I initially started asking questions about the qualifications and procedures for applying but could not get a straight answer from anyone. It seemed to be one of the biggest mysteries of the city. After about three years of being run from one political organization or another, I learned that it was going to cost me "about one thousand dollars."

I made the connection with a former city councilman who told me the truth: I was to meet with and deliver the money (cash only) to an East Chicago police detective at his house while he was on duty. I did, and in less than a month, on my twenty-fourth birthday, August 1, 1968, I reported to the police station to be sworn in to the department.

I spent the majority of my time on the police department in the Criminal Investigation Division as a homicide investigator. Two homicide cases mentioned in this book were murders that I was very familiar with. The Henry "Babe" Lopez case was actually a Hammond Police Department case because his body was found in his East Chicago city-owned car but submerged on the Hammond side of the Grand Calumet River, near the Kennedy Avenue bridge. The other case, involving Jay Given, was an East Chicago homicide, and I was the lead investigator. (There is more on my role in this case later in the book.)

I grew up in East Chicago from the tender age of six after my family arrived in 1950 from our hometown, Cayey, Puerto Rico. We came to live in one of the most notorious neighborhoods in the city and witnessed many disturbances in front of the tavern next door to our building. After watching East Chicago police officers in action, restoring peace in the neighborhood, I made up my mind that one day I would be a peacemaker.

Sixteen and a half years after becoming an officer, I was appointed chief of police. It was a total shock to me and almost everyone else in the department because I considered myself one of the least political members. After all those years on the police department, I thought I had learned a lot about East Chicago politics, but after just a few weeks as chief, I found I hadn't even scratched the surface.

It didn't take very long after my appointment before I started receiving calls from politicians asking for special "favors" or "consideration" of special treatment for "connected" people involved in a variety of illegal practices. One call in particular came after our department, along with the Indiana State Police, raided a huge gaming operation, closed several illegal "after-hour" bars and rounded up about one dozen prostitutes working the bars on Michigan Avenue. It should be noted that one of those prostitutes had solicited the mayor in broad daylight at that site when the mayor was giving a potential business investor a tour of our city. Needless to say, the mayor was not too pleased with the situation.

I served in the capacity of chief of police for five years. Several incidents that took place in that five-year span took their toll on me, both emotionally and physically, convincing me five years was enough. Let me offer an example.

In February 1988, several East Chicago police officers, including one of my high school classmates and a fellow member of our high school basketball team, were arrested on drug charges by the Drug Enforcement Administration (DEA), assisted by our internal affairs officers. Later that same year, I underwent open heart surgery. Although I remained on the job for a little over a year after that, I knew it was time to get out. And so I did, in January 1990.

Looking back, I still remain grateful for the many opportunities it afforded me. I owe so much to the mayors, police chiefs and all the honest, hardworking police officers who taught me so much and helped shape my career and my character as a public servant. We, the members of my department, did a lot of great things, and we did them together. For that, I will be forever grateful, in spite of the fact that I endured some hardships and was disappointed that the city that meant so much to me didn't live up to my expectations.

In regard to this book's content, the most important characteristic of a storyteller, in my opinion, is the author's credibility. Jerry Davich's account of public corruption in Lake County, Indiana, is believable because he is a man of high morals and character. And I am personally aware of the vast amount of research he has put into this story. The story loses all value if the teller can't be believed.

With that said, I firmly believe that the decline of East Chicago—and much of Lake County—has resulted as much due to public corruption as the decline of the steel industry. I believe this to be true based on personal observations and conversations I've had over the years with East Chicago business owners and potential investors who opted out of East Chicago.

One of the main complaints from business operators is what they termed "unwanted, silent partners," referring to city politicians who were hitting them up for high-priced political fundraising tickets or free goods and services. They also complained about regulatory divisions of the city, such as health inspectors, building department inspectors and code enforcement officers, who also had their hands in the business owners' pockets.

Potential investors, especially those from other parts of the country who were unfamiliar with the area and researched our history, were scared away by stories of the long line of politicians indicted for public corruption.

Almost a half century after becoming a police officer, I am no longer naïve about such practices in East Chicago and Lake County. Both became an upside-down world where wrong was right and right was wrong. If you didn't go along with that mentality, you couldn't be trusted. My wife, my sons and I still pray for our city and political leaders.

It's my hope that this book serves the public by educating, entertaining or enlightening readers who may also be naïve or who simply need a somber reminder about political corruption in our region—in the past and in the present.

AUGUSTO "GUS" FLORES JR.
Former East Chicago police chief

Augusto Flores Jr. joined the army in 1962 and the East Chicago police force in 1968. He earned a bachelor's degree in criminal justice from Calumet College. Augusto retired from the police department in 1990 after serving his last five years as chief of police. In 2005, he returned to work for the city after George Pabey became mayor and also returned to the police department as chief of police in 2009 before retiring in 2012.

Preface

For more than a century, northwest Indiana residents have had a deep animosity—and an even deeper fascination—with the Calumet region's infamous politicians, elected officials and public officeholders who have been convicted of public corruption.

It's a lengthy, shameful list of shady, crooked and, ultimately, disgraced politicians who have lost public trust through their dirty deeds. Our region's disdain and disappointment goes back several decades, with elected officials who have truly lived down to our statewide reputation as "region rats." This ongoing cesspool of muddied politics wreaks a stench across the rest of the state and, worse yet, around the country.

In particular, Lake County boasts a population of nearly half a million people and has become synonymous with dirty politics from the city of East Chicago—considered ground zero in this region for public corruption—to Lake Station, which recently lost big in a high-stakes scandal involving the city's gambling mayoral family.

Familiar names abound for elected officeholders who got caught with their fingers in the taxpayers' cookie jar. Here is a short list: Roswell O. Johnson, George Chacharis, Rudy Bartolomei, Vince Kirrin, Metro Holovachka, Orval Anderson, Noah Atterson Spann, Peter Manous, George Pabey, Thomas Philpot and Keith Soderquist. The full list includes so many more.

It's as if any given year wouldn't be complete in northwest Indiana without another public corruption indictment, trial and conviction. For tens of thousands of region residents who have lived through too many political scandals to count, it's not if, but when the next one will be unearthed by federal authorities. It's not a matter of who, but who else this time. The year 2016 was no different. Whispered rumors are always swirling, and possible indictments are always looming in regard to current elected officials who may soon be added to that list of shame.

You would think our elected officials wouldn't be so brazen or arrogant, considering our region's reputation, right? You'd think wrong. No-nonsense federal agents are always sniffing around local government offices, looking for something, anything, to mount a case. Sometimes, the agents leave with boxes of legal documents or public records. Other times, they leave with only the continued threat of another indictment coming down.

As the old adage goes, "You can indict a ham sandwich," meaning an indictment against an alleged criminal doesn't always mean a conviction. This is true. In Lake County, however, most every federal indictment goes down in the courtroom as surely as a beer and brat at the corner tavern. Sadly, it's still one of the few Indiana counties where the term "public service" is too often viewed as an oxymoron.

Maybe I've lived in this region for too long. Maybe I've become immune to political corruption in Lake County, always expecting the worse from its public servants. Or maybe I've come to expect elected officials from certain cities to be involved in yet another scandal, eventually. Shame on me? No, shame on those crooks. And shame on voters who repeatedly elect these types of white-collar criminals into office and then look the other way while cookies from our coffers are being heisted. Again and again and again.

There are many reasons why this region is chained to a primal form of tribal politics, spearheaded by too many "leaders" whose finest talent is their charm, whose greatest skill is racketeering and whose highest education is how to elude prosecution. By the way, if you're not exactly sure about the definition of, say, *racketeering*, or any other related terms, I'm including a handy-dandy glossary in this book. Each word, from *bribes* to *wiretapping*, has been used ad nauseam by federal agents in reference to our region's crooked politicians and their dirty deeds.

What exactly did they do? How did they do it? Why did they do it? When and where did they do it? This book will give you a crash course refresher, with candid insights from several sources who are all too familiar with public corruption in this blighted corner of our state.

As one longtime political consultant told me during a clandestine meeting in a quiet, empty bar, "It's a cultural, geographical and generational disgrace that began a century ago and has shamelessly slithered into the twenty-first century."

Acknowledgements

This book would not have been possible without the invaluable contributions from many northwest Indiana residents, some through public recordings and others through personal confessions.

Although I have been in the newspaper business for more than twenty years and have covered my share of political corruption in the Calumet region, I was not prepared for the startling history of misdeeds and misconduct at the hands of our trusted public officials. Too many sources to name here revealed name after name, crime after crime.

When I began this weighty project, I wasn't sure where to start, so, of course, I first approached Steve McShane at the Calumet Archives at Indiana University Northwest. His knowledge of this region's history—the highlights, the lowlights and its darkest secrets—never ceases to amaze me.

Also, thanks to Cal Bellamy from the Shared Ethics Advisory Commission for his insights, and to John Petalas, Thomas McDermott Jr., Thomas Vanes, Kim Frizzell, Chris Anderson, Christopher Meyers, Marie Eisenstein, Kendall Svengalis and Gus Flores, who also penned the foreword for this book. And special thanks to Joey Lax-Salinas, whose immense talents as a photographer added contemporary visuals to complement so many black-and-white historic images.

Thanks also to all the helpful employees from this region's many public libraries, especially Marla Spann from the East Chicago Public Library, for not hesitating to answer the oddest questions and strangest requests. And a special acknowledgement goes to all those unnamed political insiders who provided whispered insights, undercover meetings and dusty documents for my research and reporting and certain federal agents who offered a wealth of truly expert knowledge and priceless files. The most precious gift anyone can offer is their time. For this, I am indebted to these individuals.

A very special thanks to Lois E. Bell, whose keen interest in this topic compelled her to compile reams of historic documents, obscure paperwork and dusty publications, with many of those materials finding their way into my hands and—thankfully—my research. Lois's fingerprints can be found on many pages within this book, which became an unexpected beneficiary of her timeless efforts to document the complex and exhaustive history of this subject in northwest Indiana. Thank you, Lois.

Introduction

Public corruption: A crime involving a breach of public trust and/or abuse of position by federal, state or local officials and their private sector accomplices.

Steel mill barons and other entrepreneurs converged at the southern tip of Lake Michigan for good reason at the turn of the twentieth century. It seemed an ideal location to build factories along the lakeshore, to house workers in nearby towns, to produce endless tons of steel and, of course, to make a tidy profit for stockholders. Plus, it was the perfect location in proximity to Chicago for its big-city perks while avoiding the Windy City's blowhard politics. The plan worked to perfection, except for that last part.

Chicago's infamous reputation for shady elected officials, rampant public corruption and rough-and-tumble politics soon seeped over the state line into—appropriately named—East Chicago, Indiana. The two cities shared not only a name but also an identity that stretched from Illinois into Indiana like a pickpocket's hand into an innocent bystander's purse.

In no time, public corruption became a familiar buzz phrase in East Chicago, as well as in other Lake County cities, such as Gary and Hammond. This hardscrabble, urbanized area in the northern part of the county created a kind of Bermuda Triangle for crooked politics. Unfortunately, an ungodly amount of taxpayer dollars disappeared there over several decades. It was never recovered.

Elected officeholders and public servants who were sworn to serve, protect and uphold our laws instead conducted backroom deals with street thugs, white-collar criminals and deep-pocketed businessmen. Some of these elected officials got caught. Others slipped through the cracks of the U.S. justice system. At least one high-profile former mayor escaped conviction and jail time, but his legacy has been imprisoned in shame ever since he left office.

Some historians believe the true beginning of public corruption in Lake County took place with John Dillinger—the infamous Depression-era gangster—and his notorious escape from the Lake County Jail in Crown Point. His chummy relationship with certain law enforcement officials in 1934 was captured in a now iconic photo of a grinning Dillinger arm in arm with Lake County prosecuting attorney Robert Estill. Other historians go back even further to Chicago mobster Al Capone and his gang, which had a heavy influence in this region's crooked politics. Still, other observers trace our region's corruption to its earliest agricultural days before big industry became its cash cow.

Crooked Politics in Northwest Indiana traces our region's deep history with public corruption while fast-forwarding to modern-day convictions. By doing so, this book is similar to my previous book, *Lost Gary, Indiana*, bridging our past to our present while offering a peek at our future.

As I write these words, former Lake Station mayor Keith Soderquist still awaits sentencing for his public corruption conviction, which is outlined in a subsequent chapter in this book. Will Soderquist's conviction and sentencing serve as a warning to other elected officials currently in office who may be involved in similar crimes at this very moment? Probably not, as history has taught us.

Greed, ego and arrogance often trump doing the right thing when no one is watching, which is the very definition of ethics.

Why do some of these officeholders gamble with such high stakes knowing full well they could be caught with their hands in the public's kitty? This intriguing issue also is examined in this book from several different perspectives, not only from a jaded newspaper columnist who has learned to trust no one, especially politicians.

This book's sources include county officials, former police chiefs, local historians, defense attorneys, political consultants, research librarians, political science professors, veteran journalists and current elected officials. Together, they weave a tapestry of insights, anecdotes and possible explanations as to why this region—and especially Lake County—has been poisoned by this scourge of crime.

Other invited sources make a solid case in defense of this region's elected officeholders, citing a reputation that has been overhyped and unfairly exaggerated, they claim. Some of the public servants who have been convicted of criminal acts didn't deserve to be dragged through the mud of their predecessors' dirty deeds, according to their supporters. They have been pinched by the feds for relatively minor offenses, compared to other white-collar criminals and corporate thieves in this state, they insist.

In recent years, several indictments have been issued by this area's U.S. district attorney, followed by splashy newspaper headlines, laborious court hearings and eventual jail time for public servants who insist they have done nothing wrong. Until, that is, they later admit their guilt in an attempt to reduce their looming prison time.

Some of these corrupt politicians—or "pols" (another glossary term), as they are known—have hidden behind the Bible after being charged. Others have claimed they were wrongly marginalized in this region, so they did what they had to do to climb the ladder of success. Many of them obviously knew they were committing serious crimes, yet after being apprehended by authorities, they defended their actions through delusion or became intoxicated by bottomless rationalizations.

Many of the old-world Europeans, including my ancestors, who immigrated to this region during the early part of the last century, felt that anything was negotiable in life. Anything. This bargain basement attitude oozed into their workplace under the wink-and-nod rule: "You do something for me and I do something for you." Because everything seemed to be negotiable in life, this evolved into negotiating for, say, city jobs and work in the political world. Back in the day, these old-school pols may not have readily understood the word *nepotism*, but they clearly lived by it and flourished through it.

This included my own grandfather George Davich, a Gary official whose infamous reputation of accepting bribes, kickbacks and dirty money tarnished our family's name. It also brought him power, albeit briefly, which is the true aphrodisiac for most officeholders who turn corrupt.

They simply, and stupidly, can't say no to their lust for power, regardless of its price.

Part I

Crooked Politics in the Calumet Region

Why has Lake County been such a cesspool for rampant political corruption for more than a century? Is it due to the county boasting a one-party Democratic rule for too long? Is it a cultural phenomenon, dating back to the early political leaders of our highly industrialized area with the heavy

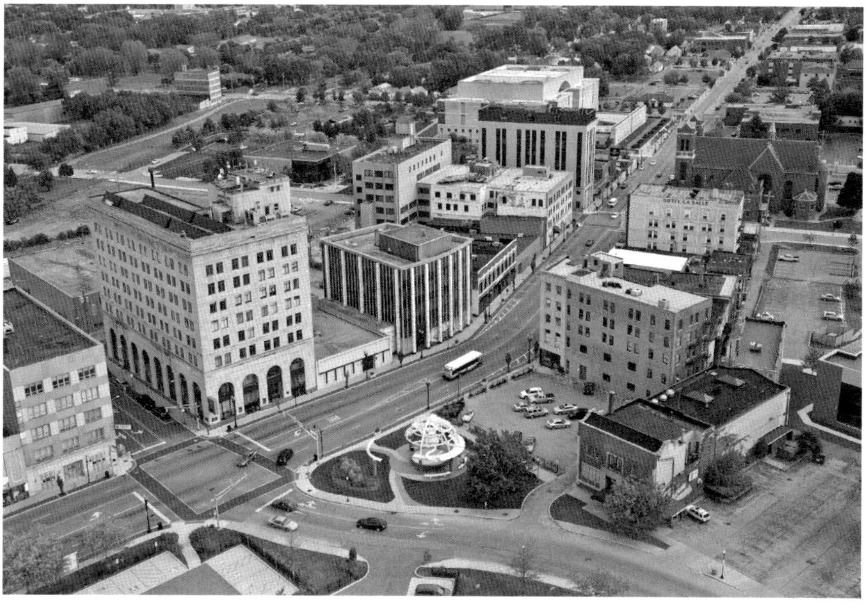

Aerial view of downtown Hammond, Indiana. *Courtesy of Joey Lax-Salinas.*

influx of tax money? Or does our geographical location—a marginalized region between the mega-metropolis of Chicago and the Hoosier holy land of Indianapolis—play a pivotal role? It can't be denied that our region is located on an island, of sorts, influenced by Chicago politics more than Hoosier values.

"Obviously, there is not just one single answer," said Marie Eisenstein, associate professor of political science at Indiana University Northwest in Gary. "I would suggest that the role of location has to do with being a more urban area than the rest of Indiana, where a political machine can, and does, successfully operate," she said. "Thus, we are influenced by Chicago because that, too, is an urban area where a party machine can be successful."

Basically, machine politics has historically manifested itself in larger cities across the country. It is used to control the benefits of public office, such as patronage, services, contracts, protection and so on. "Our location has lent itself to being more of a large urban area than a smaller one," Eisenstein said. "This is most important in terms of location."

The "Chicago machine," also called the Democrat machine, is at play in Lake County, Indiana, as much as it is in the city of Chicago, she noted.

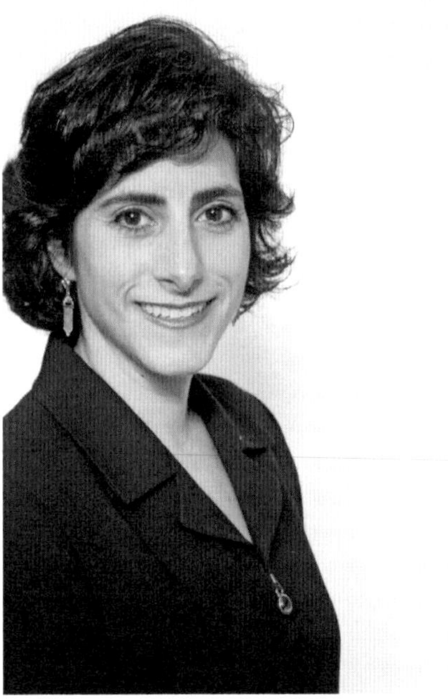

Marie Eisenstein, associate professor of political science at Indiana University Northwest in Gary. *Courtesy of Marie Eisenstein.*

"East Chicago was not just a name," she said. "It reflected doing politics in the same style as Chicago politics. Northwest Indiana is probably a unique case study unto itself."

And it worked to perfection for decades, partly because how our local government was structured, some public officials say.

"Part of the reason Lake County, in particular, is rampant with corruption is the fact that Lake County is split into so many different municipalities, each with their own competing agendas," said Hammond mayor Thomas McDermott Jr.

Lake County municipalities, together boasting roughly 480,000 residents, include Hammond, Gary, East Chicago, Whiting, Merrillville,

Hobart, Lake Station, New Chicago, Highland, Munster, Dyer, Schererville, Griffith, Crown Point, St. John, Lowell and Cedar Lake.

"Think about that," McDermott said. "We have seventeen municipalities in a county of only 480,000 people. Some of these municipalities are led by a group of council members while others are led by a mayor, such as Hammond, Gary, East Chicago, Whiting, Lake Station and Hobart. Getting seventeen municipalities onto a single agenda is nearly impossible."

Making matters worse, each municipality also is split into competing agendas. Hammond alone has several governmental entities, and each is autonomous, McDermott pointed out.

These include the civil city (led by the mayor and a nine-member city council); the school city (led by a school superintendent and a five-member school board); the township (led by trustees, assessors and a three-member board); the county (one county commissioner and a county councilman from Hammond); the library board (a superintendent and a five-member board); the state government (two state representatives and two state senators); and the federal government (led by a U.S. congressman), McDermott said.

"With this many layers and elected officials, it's hard even for the most seasoned politician to keep them all straight," McDermott said. "We have too many layers and too many decision-makers to ever have a chance to think regionally, as some would wish we would do. For members of the general public, the vast majority of them don't have a clue who represents them. So, when many of them vote, they vote simply for names they recognize. In northwest Indiana, with the way our government was structured in the 1840s, we were destined to fail," he concluded.

And destined to suffer from corruption, I might add.

In many ways, our region's political climate is similar to long-established industrial cities such as Chicago, Baltimore and Philadelphia, according to Calvin Bellamy, president of the Northwest Indiana Shared Ethics Advisory Commission. "They were populated by recent immigrants who needed basic social services," he said. "From that dependence grew political machines to meet people's needs. That seems a lot like Lake County, Indiana. We did not develop as a lake-centered resort area. Instead, the big industrialists like Rockefeller, Carnegie and Pullman wanted to be in the Chicago market but with less oversight and more open space. So they built their refineries, mills and factories here and, with them, also came the culture."

As time passed, big industry became the major taxpayer in northern Lake County.

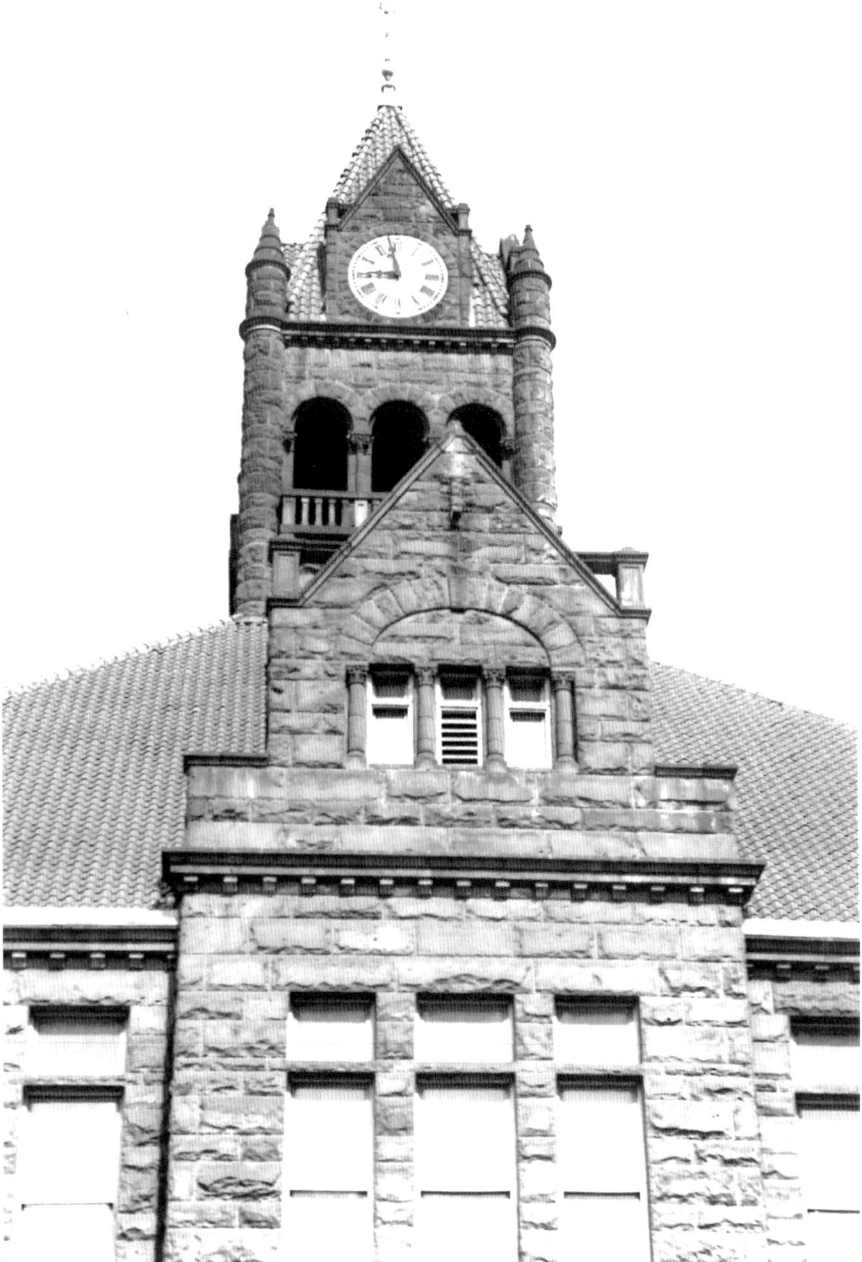

Lake County Superior Courthouse bell tower, 1920. *Courtesy of East Chicago Public Library.*

"As long as Inland Steel and Youngstown Sheet and Tube paid more than 90 percent of the property taxes in East Chicago, and U.S. Steel was the major source of revenue for Gary, the system worked pretty well," Bellamy said. "Lavish spending on public works—with an appropriate cut for the right officials—provided jobs and other services that greatly benefited the public."

This was illustrated perfectly in East Chicago during the long mayoral run of the late Robert Pastrick, when the city boasted highly impressive school buildings. Other public buildings also were large and tastefully designed, though overpriced. Plus, East Chicago residents enjoyed twice-weekly trash pickup.

"Life was good and mostly free for the average citizen," Bellamy said.

Mostly free financially, anyway. Such municipal amenities came with a cost, which were historically billed at the ballot box on Election Day.

"Pastrick's mayoral chief of staff once told me that all the talk about efficiency and staff reductions was misplaced," Bellamy said. "He said, 'You need to understand, if the city didn't hire these people, they wouldn't be able to get jobs anywhere else.' I think he was proud that the city was able to help people in this way, and of course, in return those folks were expected to vote the right way—just like in Chicago, Philadelphia and Baltimore. This perfect match of mutual self-interest worked until property tax reform, which shifted the real estate tax burden from businesses to homeowners. But, by then, the culture was established and it would not die easily."

It still hasn't died in Lake County.

Jim Flannery, former executive director of the Northwest Indiana Quality of Life Council, also blames systemic corruption on an overall complacency by the electorate. "Under the Democratic Party banner, there is a continuing mantra of it being the party of the little guys, versus the big corporate enemy in the Republican Party," he said. "There also is a culture of entitlement where the good guys will take care of the people with perks, jobs and influence, when needed. This culture became ingrained and accepted as the way it was supposed to be, and any change would not be for the good."

Flannery came to this region from Pennsylvania as an agent for such change. He did so in part through a controversial public outreach campaign to introduce a possible replacement for the derogatory term "region rat" to describe northwest Indiana residents. Instead, Flannery suggested, region residents could be called the more upbeat and positive "Regionnaires."

"Regionnaires are concerned and engaged citizens who love northwest Indiana and aspire to be leaders in transforming the culture and perceptions

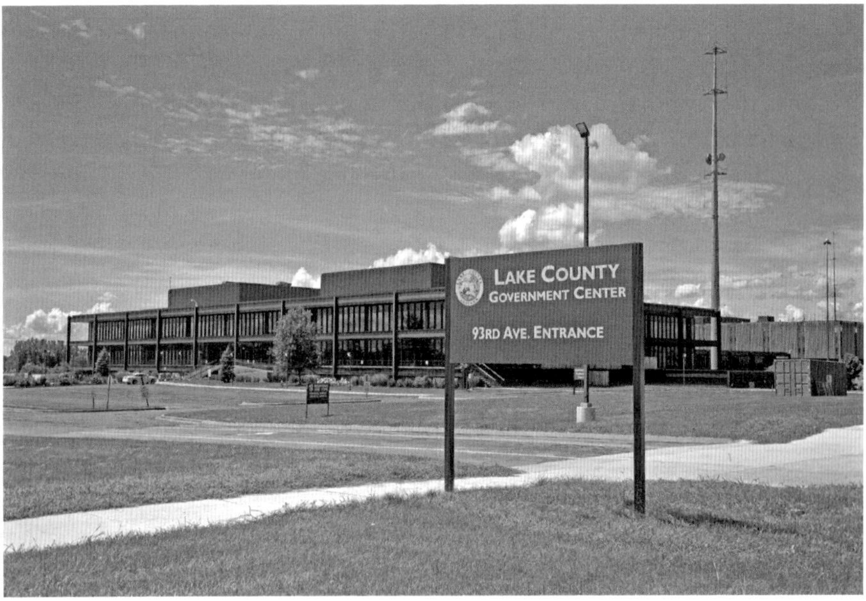

Lake County Government Complex, Crown Point, Indiana. *Courtesy of Joey Lax-Salinas.*

of this Region for the 21st Century," according to a Northwest Indiana Quality of Life Council newsletter.

"It is precisely that change that I am attempting to spark by calling out the weaknesses of the term *region rat* and the associated perceptions that go with it," Flannery told me at the time.

Northwest Indiana historian Stephen McShane, curator of the Calumet Regional Archives at Indiana University Northwest, once shared with me a theory on the origin of the outdated, but still celebrated, term. "Region rat is derived from the legends of huge rats, some as large as dogs, roaming our local steel mills and pretty much doing what they want with no fear of humans," said McShane, who noted the book *Land of the Millrats* by folklorist Richard Dorson. "Perhaps these mill rats morphed into a label for anyone from our region."

Perhaps, but whatever the term's origin, many region residents insist on wearing it like a badge of honor. Tens of thousands of longtime citizens here proudly wear the region rat reputation, and they will never see themselves as anything else, until death do them part. Not only do they feel ostracized and alienated by our own state and the Chicagoland area, but true region rats also embrace and revel in this historic marginalization.

This attitude also plays a role in the public corruption and politics-related crimes in this tiny but influential corner of the state. It doesn't matter that the deprecatory name sums us up as simple-minded, knuckle-dragging bumpkins who wallow in pollution, corruption and political shadiness.

"It is gleefully played up by those folks downstate and neighboring states to pigeonhole all of us and to impart a negative perception of all whom, unfortunately to them, have to live here," states one newsletter update from the Quality of Life Council. "That false pride is nothing more than a weak attempt to dispel the hurt and shame that others want to hand us."

Flannery, who relocated here in 1987 after a lengthy steelmaking career in Pittsburgh, was known for forward-thinking ideas that painted a fresh face on our black-eyed reputation. He was behind a series of billboards along the Borman Expressway that touted positive but little known facts about northwest Indiana. For example, Tuskegee airman Quentin P. Smith is from this region, as are four Nobel Prize laureates.

Nonetheless, changing this region's political climate is much tougher than merely changing the residents' nickname.

"As a cultural explanation, corruption is, quite simply, expected as the norm," Eisenstein said.

This norm includes backroom deals before boardroom decisions, and a cross-pollination of political cronyism. Too many politicians have felt like it's finally their turn at the helm, and because of this, they have an air of entitlement. It's the same air that's been inhaled in gasps by generations of public officeholders and aspiring candidates. In some legal circles, they call this racketeering.

In Lake County, it's called business as usual. This entitlement mindset has been passed down from generation to generation like a secret torch. To this day, this flickering spark of malfeasance continues to be passed down. It has not been extinguished, despite many attempts by federal agents, civic groups, law enforcement and local activists.

"Public corruption is not something of the past," insisted Thomas Frank, an outspoken activist from East Chicago. "Our judiciary system is subsumed by the fighting forces in our political economy. This is how and why great powerful wrongs go unaddressed."

Such powerful wrongs have caused disillusionment and disappointments for too many voters who have showed an affinity for false political prophets. These voters have willingly or stupidly believed the lies behind the politicians' criminal behavior. Because of this, too many influential politicians have been

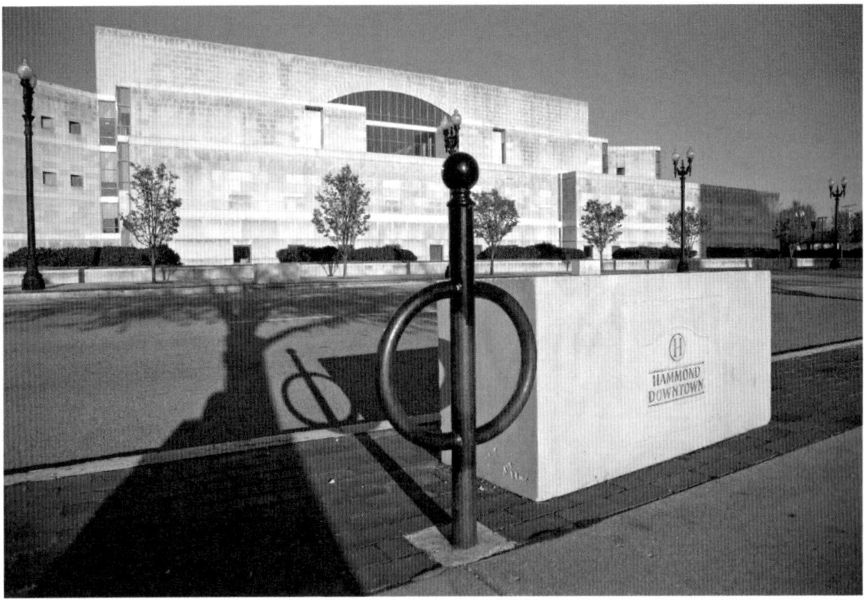

U.S. District Court Federal Courthouse, Hammond, Indiana, side view. *Courtesy of Joey Lax-Salinas.*

treated like rock stars, with the current generation experiencing the tail end of such expected privilege.

"Most of the Democratic and Republican machines have faded from existence," Eisenstein said. "Chicago has held on the longest, and so has northwest Indiana."

Keep in mind that today's machine politics and one-party rule are nothing like the powerful machines between the 1870s and 1940s, she noted.

"I am not sure there was ever a heyday for public corruption in Lake County," Eisenstein said. "In the early days, such as the 1930s and on, the Democratic Party was so flush with economic money in Lake County that no one seemed to care or notice that so much was skimmed by so many. It only became an issue starting in the 1970s when the economics stopped being as lucrative as it had been historically. The most that can be said is that because of the changed economy, the nature of corruption has changed. But not the fact that it is still occurring. Now, corruption centers on new sources, like taxes, gambling revenue and public money, such as for public schools."

Political corruption in Lake County goes back much longer than what most residents believe. Prejudice, perception and ignorance prompt us to believe it began in previous administrations, popularized by familiar names in the news. In truth, it extends much further than you would think.

"It extends from the early 1800s until the present day," Eisenstein said. "It has historically included both Democratic and Republican machines. All machine politics was consolidated in large cities and urban centers. One-party rule is particularly pernicious. Typically, it leads to more corruption."

Essentially, the less competition that exists, the fewer adherences to democratic practices there are and the more likely there is to be corruption. Tied to the lack of political competition is a lack of economic competition, she noted.

"That is, in order to benefit economically, in an environment bereft of political competition, one must be positioned to receive favorable treatment from the party in power," Eisenstein said. "Basically, the controlling powers can bestow favorable government contracts or vigorously enforce onerous regulations to prevent new economic opportunity. All of this speaks to a failure to respect, uphold and pursue adherence to the rule of law; of being a government of laws and not 'men.'"

Historically speaking, the Democratic machine has focused on the lower socioeconomic levels of our population, more so than the Republican machine.

"Put differently, the Democratic machine attracted the immigrant and the low-level worker by providing patronage, services, contracts and protection," Eisenstein explained. "The Republican machines focus on the middle-class vote."

This adds an element of truth to the stereotypical perception that the Democratic Party is for the "little guy" or "working guy."

"To a struggling immigrant, giving your vote to the political party that will ensure you and your family are given a government job is certainly appealing. But, government jobs are not economic development," Eisenstein said, echoing what she often teaches her students.

"Our government has no independent resources of its own; it does not make and sell widgets, for example," she tells students. "It only has what it can collect from us in taxes. Thus, economically speaking, its emphasis should be on creating the environment for private industry to thrive so that more people can be employed and the government can collect the revenue it needs to support the social programs we want as a society."

"Uncontrolled patronage—based on party support and not merit-based employment—is not a legitimate system," she surmised.

Still, this most surely became the political system in this area, and in many ways, it remains in place to this day. It's just one of many factors explaining why Lake County in particular has earned its infamous and unsavory reputation. And it's why sadly, yet fittingly, political corruption *is* a science in this region.

1

Getting Intoxicated at First Political Fundraiser

In 2006, I got intoxicated at my first political fundraiser in Lake County. No, it's not what you think. I had just become the new metro columnist for the *Post-Tribune* newspaper, and I figured part of my new job involved the county's notorious political beat. So, armed with my pen, notepad and a bottomless cocktail of naiveté, I pulled in to the jammed parking lot at the (now closed) Patio restaurant in Merrillville. For many years, the popular joint served as a watering hole for generations of Lake County politicians. Here's my column from that unforgettable evening, which turned into a true baptism by fire.

I figure there's no way all these cars are here for "An Evening with Lake County Treasurer John E. Petalas."

I mean who the heck is John E. Petalas? And do insiders merge together his first name and middle initial to call him "John-ny"? Or do they call him "The Treasurer." And should I, too, to appear like I belong?

And who attends these hoity-toity political fundraisers anyway? Certainly not the hoi polloi, i.e. you and me. With donations starting at $100 a pop—I got in with a complimentary ticket—I figure most of these cars came for the off-track betting parlor next door, right? Wrong.

The Patio's banquet hall is packed with political officials, political wannabes, and political sycophants. I, on the other hand, am a political virgin, a sheep in a wolf's clothing, a columnist with a million other places to be on this Friday night.

I don't know any pols. I don't use pols as unnamed sources. I don't yuck it up with pols after hours. Heck, this is the first time I ever wrote "pols" instead of politicians.

Besides the female servers here—"Yes, can I please get a Coke on the rocks"—I'm probably the only person who doesn't want something from somebody for some favor or some fee or for some friend of a friend. No, wait, I'm here for a column. So indict me.

Well anyway, I'm standing at the wide open bar next to an old-timer named E. Hugh McLaughlin. The 78-year-old former Gary city councilman has a bottle of Miller Lite in one hand and an endless Parliament cigarette in the other.

"Does the smoke bother you?" he asks, surveying the room for familiar faces.

"Nah," I say, lying, sliding slightly away from him.

The Hobart man also used a free ticket to get in, with plans to make the most of it. He arrived at 6 p.m. sharp, he already downed three beers, and he keeps eyeing the food buffet line.

"You gotta try the fish here," he keeps telling me. "It's the best."

During my hour here, no less than five people tell me to try the fish. I don't like fish.

Even though I was born and raised in Lake County, I've never been to Friday night fish fries or anything involving politics. I know, I'm satanic. Consider me the anti-E. Hugh McLaughlin, who seems to know everybody here.

"You see him," he says, nodding toward a well-dressed middle-aged guy with graying hair and a polished smile. "Yeah, he's an honest guy," McLaughlin tells me.

"You see him," nodding to another guy, "not so honest."

(By the way, this describes most guys here, and many whip out business cards from their crisp suits like a pistol from a holster.)

I recognize only three elected officials, one who ignores me (Karen, what gives?), and another who says he enjoys my columns. Should I believe him? The rest are strangers.

Hobart attorney David Gilyan tells me these events are all alike, like "Groundhog Day." "You haven't missed a damn thing," he says.

Andrew Kyres, a banking guy and a Crown Point city councilman, invites me to his table for dinner. Very kind. I decline.

Then I meet Randy Palmateer, from Local Electricians Union 697, who I shouldn't like. Oh, not for his politics but because he's the guy who won that St. Jude House home raffle earlier this year. I started picking kitchen colors the week before the drawing.

I eventually shake hands with John E. Petalas, who I end up calling "sir." He seems like a nice man, an honest man, an appreciative man who thanks guests in triplicate.

Before the band begins, Gary Mayor Rudy Clay takes the stage, telling guests that "God is a democrat." I think he believes it. He then slams Republican congressmen who send out pornographic e-mails. "We don't do none of that," he preaches.

To my right, an elderly man ignores Clay's speech and instead overfills a paper plate with choice desserts. He covers it with a napkin and slips out the door. Smart man, I tell myself.

Before I leave, sans the desserts, McLaughlin waves over several more guys, introducing me like we're long-time pals. After a while, I feel like his long-time pal. In fact, I feel like a long-time pal to most everyone I meet.

It's an intoxicating feeling. I stagger outside, wander to my car, and try sobering up.

Well, it's been ten years since I attended that political fundraiser. I've since been to many more of them for various candidates. I've also gotten to better know some of those elected officials I mentioned, including former Gary mayor Rudy Clay, who has since passed away. McLaughlin also passed away, but he kept in contact with me regularly since we first met at this fundraiser.

In hindsight, David Gilyan, the Hobart attorney who now lives in Las Vegas, was right. They're all alike, just like in the movie *Groundhog Day*—same purpose, same unspoken rules, same political chit-chat under the guise of polite conversation. Only the faces change and sometimes the hairstyles. Sometimes not. Attending these never-ending affairs—designed to fill campaign coffers and make new political connections—is often like walking into a time capsule. Without much effort, it's easy to pretend these events are being held in, say, 2006 or 1986 or 1956.

In Lake County, Indiana, it's always fashionable to be seen at these fundraisers because pols know damn well it's not *what* you know—it's *who.*

2
Murders and Mysteries

Babe Lopez and Jay Given

The Murder of Henry "Babe" Lopez

On December 12, 1979, Henry "Babe" Lopez went missing under a political cloud of suspicion. Not coincidentally, his city-owned 1977 Oldsmobile was reported stolen that same day.

How? Why? Where? People are still talking about this notoriously political case nearly forty years later.

Lopez was a family man and loyal friend, according to those who knew him. He was active in civic duties in and around East Chicago, Indiana. He was a board member of the Northwest Indiana Health Services and president of the Indiana Harbor Little League. He sponsored bowling teams and Little League baseball teams.

Lopez was also a generous man, reaching for his wallet to dole out spare cash to those in need, according to friends and family. He cared deeply for his community and his loved ones, news accounts state.

Everything, though, wasn't rainbows and lollipops in Lopez's complex political life.

Weeks before his disappearance, Lopez had a feeling that something bad was going to go down, according to several newspaper stories published after his disappearance. He began covering his tracks and watching his back. At one point, he asked his son to make copies of several city parks department

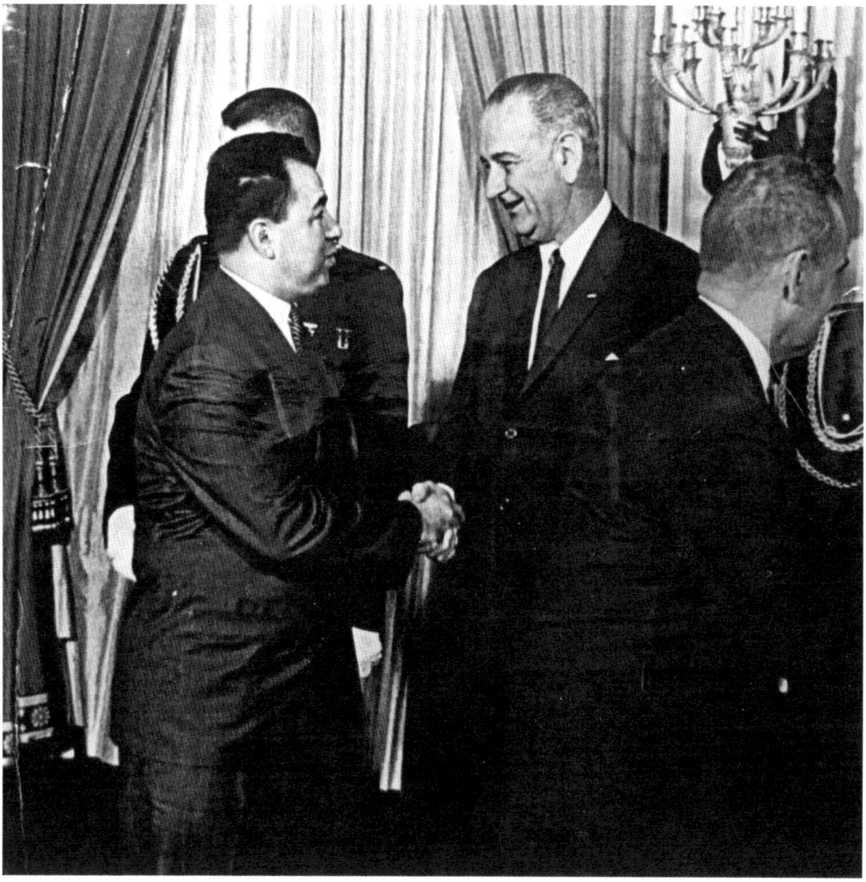

Henry "Babe" Lopez with Lyndon B. Johnson. *Courtesy of Calumet Regional Archives.*

records and keep them out of sight, according to police records. He also made odd requests for friends to care for his wife, Norma, if anything happened to him. He even asked friends to wear leather jackets when they were around him, to appear as if he had bodyguards, police say. Lopez had also been receiving threatening phone calls.

Why would such an unassuming character, at least in appearance, be so worried for his safety? He had something to hide—as too many officials do in this region—something involving ill-gotten money and powerful connections. In 1974, before Lopez became East Chicago parks superintendent, the city council transferred $900,000 into the parks budget, reportedly under a line item that didn't exist, police say. No one could tell police how that money was spent in detail. In 1977, while Lopez was in office, he secured city council approval to use $145,000 of that fund to cover salaries for employees in his department. From 1977 to 1983, the Indiana State Board of Accounts repeatedly questioned how the park bond money had been spent. The state agency questioned then–city controller James Knight to determine if the funds had been used for its intended purpose. Due in part to that investigation, Knight suspended Lopez on December 11, 1979, the day before he disappeared, court records show.

This wasn't the only infraction of which Lopez had been accused, according to a December 14, 2009 story in the *Times* newspaper. In 1980, former East Chicago mayor Robert Pastrick told Hammond police that he considered replacing Lopez. "I started losing faith in his performance," Pastrick told police. "He just wasn't doing his job, quite frankly."

The mayor noted that Lopez put too many employees on the payroll, overspent his department's bloated budget and allegedly received kickbacks from a city vendor, the story stated. "He had guys on the payroll over there that weren't even working," Pastrick told police. "He had all kinds of shit going on over there."

Records show that state auditors also cited Lopez for not turning in fees collected for parking and buoy rentals. Police said his family was asked after his death to repay $9,575 in missing rental funds.

Pastrick also told authorities that Lopez was not turning in collections for the mayor's special "2 percent" fund, according to the 130-page police report. This fund came from employees' paychecks, and the percentage was automatically deducted and deposited into campaign coffers of elected officials.

Meanwhile, after Lopez's mysterious disappearance, weeks passed with no answers, no credible leads and no dead body found.

On January 29, 1980, law enforcement officials sent a dive team into the Grand Calumet River to look for a crash victim's submerged vehicle. Instead, the dive team found under the murky waters Lopez's city-owned 1977 Oldsmobile. Its municipal license plate was caked with mud and suspicion. No sooner than you can say "sleeps with the fishes," divers found Lopez's body in the driver's seat, a gunshot wound to his neck, likely from someone in the backseat. Lopez's left arm was propped outside the driver's side window, a gold-plated watch still on his wrist. On the car's floorboard, divers found a large rock near the gas pedal.

Law enforcement agencies focused their attention on Edelmiro "Corfi" DeJesus for Lopez's death, based on tips. But DeJesus, an alleged mob hit man involved in numerous illegal activities, was killed execution-style on May

27, 1980, four months after Lopez's body was found in the river. According to police, DeJesus was likely killed because he boasted about killing Lopez.

Police believed someone else, however, ordered the hit on Lopez, and that someone could have been Vince Kirrin, a longtime political operative in Lake County, police say. It was an unspoken rule that nothing political was allowed in East Chicago without Kirrin's approval or the backroom blessing from former East Chicago mayor Robert Pastrick, who served in office amid the murders of Lopez and Jay Given, in 1981.

Kirrin was never convicted for Lopez's death, but he was indicted for public corruption during a federal investigation. He served time in prison and died in 1998.

After Lopez's murder, Hammond police detectives Dave Moulesong and Steve Summers were ordered to investigate the highly controversial case. They vigorously followed leads, laboriously interviewed sources and, somewhere along the line, obviously rattled too many cages in East Chicago. In July 1980, they were ordered to stop their investigation and wrap up their paperwork, despite their objections.

Somebody, from somewhere, made the decision to take the case out of the Hammond police officers' hands. The case never made it to the prosecutor's

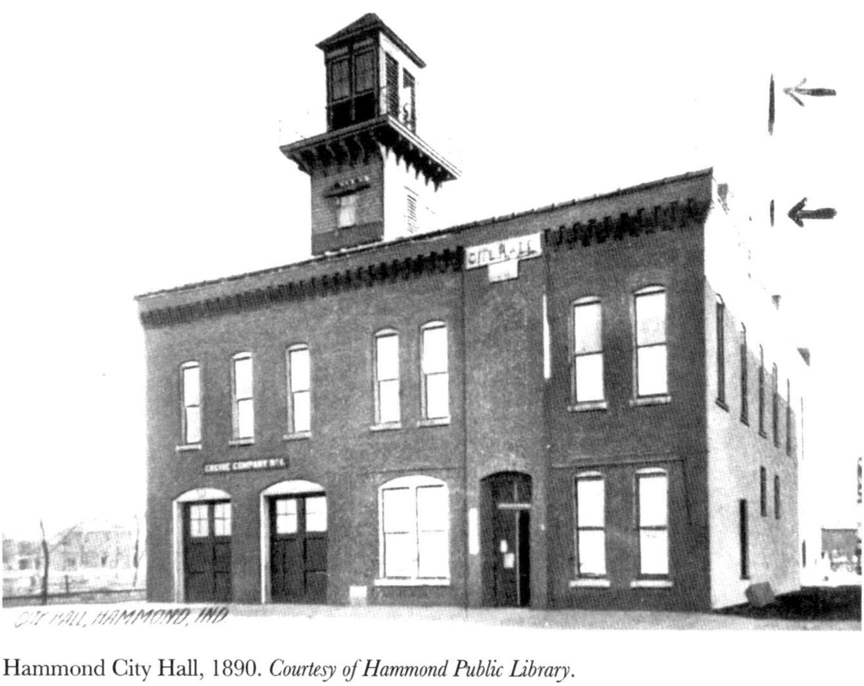

Hammond City Hall, 1890. *Courtesy of Hammond Public Library.*

office. This is unheard of anywhere in the country for such a high-profile murder case—not in East Chicago during that era, though.

The officers were told that another law enforcement agency would handle the white-hot murder case. But no other agency followed up with it. It soon cooled off and eventually turned into a cold case, a very cold case. Due to the fact that there is no statute of limitations on murder, this case is still open, according to Hammond police.

As one veteran attorney involved in the case told me, "The case disappeared and died, just like Babe Lopez."

THE MURDER OF JAY GIVEN

Only in East Chicago can a homicide take place at a political fundraiser with four hundred guests just a room away and nobody see or hear a thing. This is precisely what happened on May 15, 1981, inside the Elks building at 4624 Magoun Avenue.

Jay Given, a fifty-one-year-old political powerbroker who was once dubbed the city's "midnight mayor" was a lot of things to a lot of people. He was a husband and father. He was a municipal attorney. He was known to make or break politicians. He had a nasty temper and made enemies as fast as he made friends, former associates agreed.

From 1963 to 1973, Given served as city attorney and then later as an advisor for East Chicago mayor Robert Pastrick. It was rumored that the two powerful politicos had a falling out years later. In fact, on the very night of his murder, Given attended a fundraiser for N. Atterson Spann, Pastrick's opponent for mayor at the time. Given may not have attended every political function in the city, but since his falling out with Pastrick, he wanted to realign himself with Spann.

As the events of the night played out, Given had just won $300 in a ticket drawing at the Las Vegas–style fundraiser in the Elks' ballroom. He had just left the room when, just after 11:00 p.m., he walked to the first-floor lobby toward the building's main entrance. One witness claimed he saw Given and a man with dark hair, wearing a dark suit, get into a heated argument as Given left the vestibule. Given had his car keys in one hand and a cigarette lighter in the other, the witness said.

Police believe this was when the dark-haired man shot Given in the back of the head at point-blank range, execution style. According to the police report, the bullet went through the back of Given's head, exited through the middle of his forehead, broke through a glass door leading outside and landed on the street, several feet away. The bullet's casing landed on the vestibule floor, police said. Given's body fell with his head lodged between the glass doors, the police report states.

At 11:14 p.m., an anonymous call came into police headquarters. A woman with a Spanish accent reported that a man had been shot. In hindsight, former East Chicago police chief Gus Flores, the primary investigator on the case, regrets that no one interviewed this female caller, who likely feared for her safety.

When the sound of the gunshot rattled through the ballroom, hundreds of guests made a mad dash out of the building. Some trampled over Given's body, tampering with potential evidence, police said. No one came forward to admit witnessing the assassination-style shooting. At one point, a Jockey Club employee, Odessa Gamble, spent ten days in jail for contempt for not cooperating with police detectives. If anyone came forward to talk to authorities, it only led to more dead ends. This was a frustrating time for investigators, left with too few witnesses and a compromised crime scene.

One key clue, however, was discovered. A bullet casing found in the building's vestibule turned out to be a match for a rare .45-caliber Detonics pistol. It was widely known around the city that East Chicago deputy police chief John Cardona owned such a handgun. No murder weapon was found and neither was Cardona's rare pistol. The deputy police chief became the prime suspect in the case, even failing a polygraph test about the homicide, but he was never charged, police say.

At the time of Given's killing, bad blood spilled across the city between Pastrick supporters and Given supporters over Cardona's suspected involvement with evidence tampering on the case. Former Lake County sheriff Stephen "Bob" Stiglich served as East Chicago police chief at the time, just as he did during the investigation for Henry Lopez. His critics have always pointed fingers in his direction, but no one was ever fingered and convicted for Given's killing.

To this day, Flores says the case still haunts him, offering a hint of hope that it can someday be solved. As one veteran attorney who worked that case put it, "It's the kind of story that only happens in Lake County, Indiana."

3
Pointing Fingers

Conservatives Blame Democratic Party Rule

It's impossible to ignore the fact that a dominant political party in Lake County, or any county, plays a crucial role in public corruption crimes.

"Rampant corruption is a complex issue but, definitely, the dominance of one party is a major factor," said Lake County historian Bruce Woods. "Whether it is Democrats or Republicans who are dominant, it creates a lack of competition and a very strong political machine."

For example, consider the city of Gary through its rags-to-riches-to-rags history.

"The second mayor of Gary was a Republican with a succession of Republican mayors after that," Woods said. "Lake County was heavily Republican at the time. Mayor R.O. Johnson served as mayor from 1914 to 1918, from 1922 to 1925 and from 1930 to 1935. In 1923, he was convicted of violating the Volstead Act. He began serving his sentence in 1925 when President Calvin Coolidge, a Republican, granted him a pardon. Johnson ran successfully two more times."

Kim Krull, a lifelong Lake County resident and retired Lake County Republican chairwoman, is convinced where there is money and power, public corruption will follow.

"When a region doesn't have oversight with at least a two-party system, it is more apt to become and remain corrupt. That's what Lake County had for many decades and why, in my opinion, it will remain that way [without] competition or oversight. Democrats have had control of local and county government for many decades. The voters have too often not had an opportunity to vote for someone other than a democrat."

Krull, who was elected as Lake County's first female political party chairman in 2009, said this is why she and other Republican officials in the county worked hard to find "qualified candidates" to run in all elected office positions.

"Of course the Democrats had such a massive machine with money and votes that it was hard to crack through," said Krull, who was elected as a Center Township board member in 2015. "An uneducated electorate is hard to break through. Add on top of that unions and [alleged] payoffs to democratic precinct committeemen, then it is almost impossible."

Krull and other conservative-leaning Republicans in this region point to a long history of machine-generated nepotism, ill-gotten job contracts and disappearing federal funds under Democratic Party rule.

"Eliminating the 'friends and family' job plan by the state legislature has helped, as has some other state legislation," Krull said. "Until we have a strong two-party system of government at every level, we will continue to fight public corruption."

Chicago's machine politics continue to play a major role in influencing this region's politics, even into 2016 and beyond, she said. "It didn't help that the Gary-Chicago Airport was not taken under control of the state to have proper funding so it could be developed into a major regional airport. It didn't help that a state bridge was condemned because it was unsafe, only to have no plan to replace it. As the state loses more and more revenue from the region due to decreased steel and refinery production, we will see even fewer tax dollars returned here."

Dan Blankenship, Cedar Creek Township board president, also strongly believes that blame should largely be pointed at the county's Democratic Party. "If more Republicans thought they had the possibility of winning office, their campaign efforts would surely uncover more questionable dealings," he said. "Freedom of Information Act requests increase when someone has skin in the game."

Blankenship cited his experience serving as a Republican chairman while helping a Republican candidate unseat a twelve-year incumbent Democrat. Blankenship said he discovered the Democratic opponent was not reporting expenditures on his campaign finance reports.

"If he didn't have an opponent in the general election, this would have never been exposed," Blankenship said. "I had hoped that things were changing when the late Hank Adams was elected as Lake County assessor,

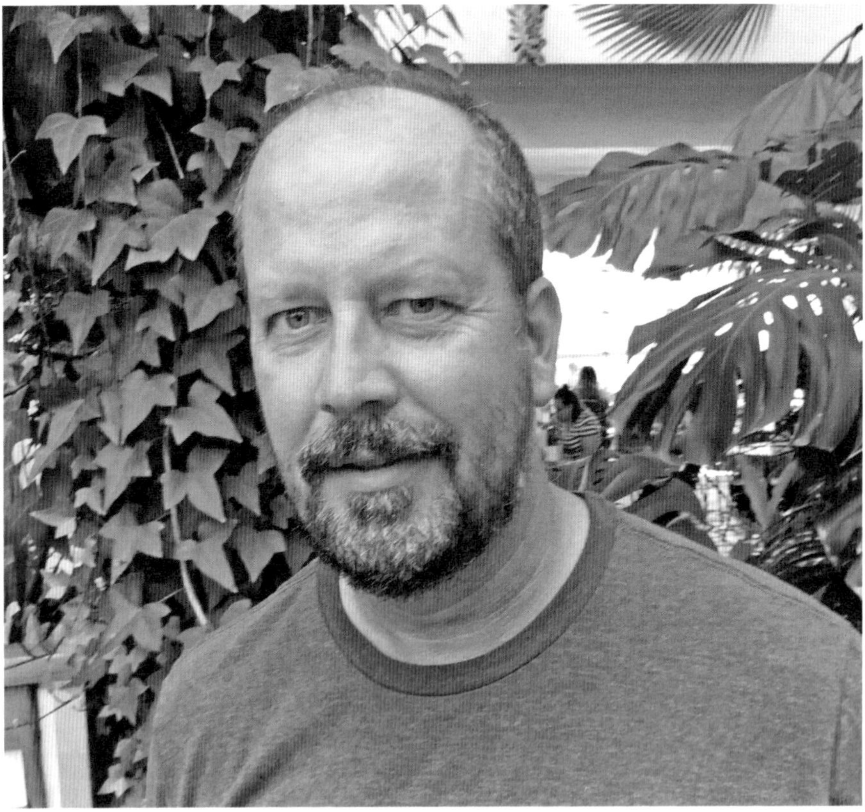

Dan Blankenship, Cedar Creek Township Board president. *Courtesy of Dan Blankenship.*

but the Democrats' stronghold on this county will always make folks wonder if we have real checks and balances."

Krull and Blankenship, among other conservatives in a largely liberal corner of the state, are confident that the Republican Party has qualified candidates for Lake County public offices.

"Professionalism should trump political clout," Blankenship insisted.

Yes, it should. But will it? Can it? Who can make such wishful thinking a reality in a county submerged in political power?

Blankenship blames voters to a degree for not taking a stand, but he also blames local media for a lack of investigative reporting into this issue.

"Simply following the money trails, the hiring practices or the pay-to-play schemes…can help change public opinion," he said. "I think we had a period during the 1970s through the 1990s when things were really bad. I think the power trip has been going on since then…when not many people were paying attention. I would like to think that some of these people really did not understand the law. Or that they had no idea what they were doing was illegal. In the extreme cases, I know that was not true. Absolute power corrupts absolutely over the top here in Lake County."

Blankenship's haunting last line echoes similar assessments from other critics of the county's political culture. Such criticism has dated back longer than you might think.

"The revelation of corruption in the public life of this community should more than shock decent citizens. There should be a surge of anger among honest, decent people of Lake County against the betrayal of public trust for personal gain. Further, the resentment must be translated into citizen action. Or do the people want to see the same old corruption, bribes, kickbacks, payoffs, public apathy?"

These timely yet timeless words were uttered by Francis E. Lynch, director of the Northwest Indiana Crime Commission. When? In 1962, the year I was born in Gary.

4

In Defense of Public Officials in "Da Region"

Like many elected officials in this region, Lake County treasurer John Petalas believes northwest Indiana has earned an unfair reputation regarding its public officeholders.

"There are hundreds of elected and appointed public officials who work in Lake County. It is not fair to label everyone a crook because of a small minority who betrayed the public trust," said Petalas, a longtime public officeholder. "Every time one of these guys gets in trouble, they make bigger headlines than a double murder investigation. The bigger the headline, the bigger the perception that all politicians are crooks."

Other veteran officials agree, making a case in defense of this area's elected officeholders who have never committed any criminal acts. They cite a reputation that has been overhyped and unfairly exaggerated over the course of more than seventy-five years.

"I don't think any elected official comes into office with the mindset that he or she will be corrupt," Petalas said. "There are some elected officials in this part of the state who went to jail for things that are completely legal for state officials to commit. There are those who feel that what they did was not wrong because their attorneys have told them so in advance."

Through the years, Petalas has personally fielded dozens of questions from members of the Indiana State Board of Accounts.

"Their reply is standard—get an opinion from your attorney and we will not find an audit exception to that opinion. Well I guess that doesn't work anymore. But then, just like in every profession, you have the dumb and

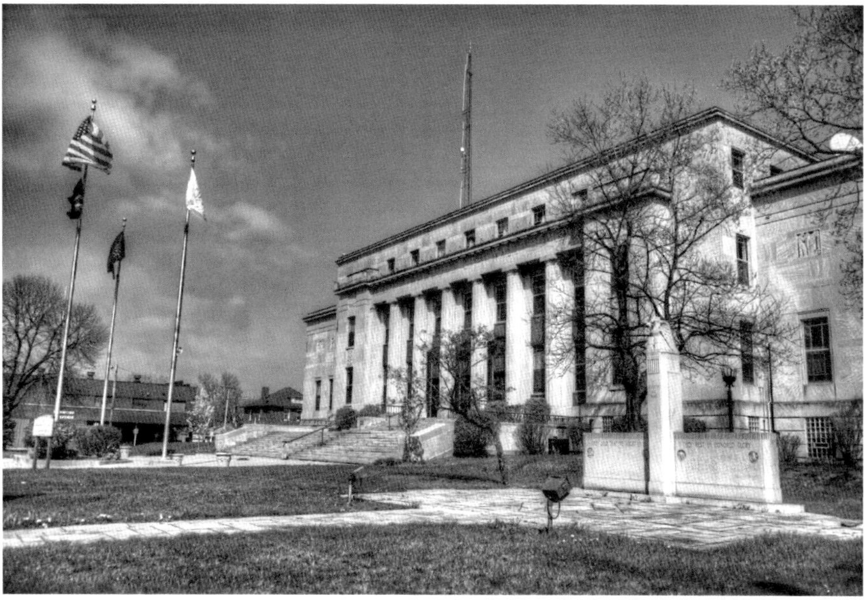

Hammond City Hall, 2016. *Courtesy of Joey Lax-Salinas.*

dumber. People who rebuild their summer homes with city products and labor. Businesspeople who are already millionaires, but who don't feel that they have enough in the bank. So they get some dumb and dumber politician to go along with their ploy and then they get caught."

Some of the public servants who have been convicted of criminal acts didn't deserve to be dragged through the mud of their predecessors' dirty deeds, according to their supporters. They have been pinched by the feds for relatively minor offenses—compared to other white-collar criminals and corporate thieves in this state and country—they insist.

"That's legal graft, isn't it?" asked Calumet region historian James Lane. "I think it's outrageous how U.S. attorneys have gone after people like Katie Hall and George Van Til for petty things—such as their staff selling candy bars or picking up a tuxedo—while millions in legal graft are siphoned into law firms for attorneys' fees."

Lane insists such indictments against "small potatoes" illegal shenanigans by certain elected officials are based off political pressure from corporate industrialists. It's no secret that public officeholders have used their staff for campaigning and reelection purposes for decades. Why have federal prosecutors singled out certain politicians but not others who also have had their hands in the taxpayers' proverbial cookie jar?

"I can only really speak about Gary, but I think the degree of corruption there is much exaggerated," Lane said. "It is true that the Democratic Party between the 1930s and 1967 was in cahoots with vice and gambling interests, but [former Gary mayor Richard] Hatcher was the most investigated mayor of his generation and he came out clean. So if they can't get to Hatcher, they get to his allies, such as Mary Elgin and Van Til. Throw the book at them and something will stick."

Is this region's political climate getting better or worse as we progress through the twenty-first century? In recent years, there have been many highly publicized indictments and eventual convictions. Still, does this mean there is more corruption taking place, or is law enforcement becoming more effective?

"I think a case can be made that it is largely the latter," replied Calvin Bellamy, president of the Shared Ethics Advisory Commission. "What used to be considered local corruption has been federalized. All of the indictments have come from the U.S. Attorney's Office. Not only are they doing more, but they seem to be catching the bad guys quicker while the malfeasance is still small time."

The Lake County Prosecutor's Office has its hands full with murders, domestic violence and other crimes. And the Indiana Attorney General's Office is more occupied with social issues, consumer fraud and other such crimes, Bellamy said.

"Ethics training can certainly help, especially in assisting basically good people to be more aware of dangerous circumstances. We can help make unethical behavior easier to recognize and perhaps even unfashionable. But someone who sets out to steal or cheat cannot be stopped that way. The U.S. attorney is the only hammer for that sort of person. The U.S. Attorney's Office is doing the heavy lifting, and I think the word has gone out to the more seasoned politicians that corruption is more dangerous than ever," Bellamy said.

Heavy lifting indeed.

The U.S. attorney is the chief federal law enforcement officer in a given district, responsible for federal criminal prosecutions and civil cases involving the federal government. In the government's Northern District of Indiana, David Capp was nominated for U.S. attorney on December 23, 2009, and confirmed by the Senate on April 22, 2010. Prior to that, Capp has served as interim U.S. attorney on three different occasions since joining the office in 1985.

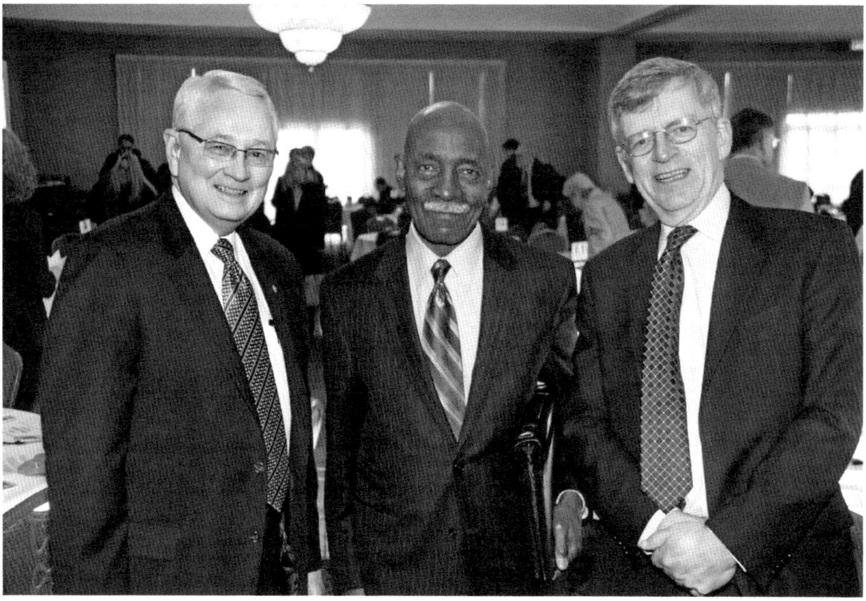

Cal Bellamy, president of Shared Ethics Advisory Commission (*left*), Indiana Supreme Court justice Robert Rucker (*center*) and U.S. attorney David Capp, Northern District of Indiana, at the 2015 Ethics Summit, on March 12, 2015, at Avalon Manor in Merrillville, Indiana. *Courtesy of Shared Ethics Advisory Commission.*

"We have a very active public corruption task force in northwest Indiana," Capp said at one of his many news conferences inside the federal courthouse in Hammond.

Under his office's initiative dubbed Operation Restore Public Integrity, more than sixty public officials have been sent to federal prison since 2001. During Capp's time at the helm, the 1968 Gary Lew Wallace High School graduate has indicted and convicted dozens of public figures on corruption charges. Region residents are rarely surprised by new indictments. It's often not a matter of if, but when the next indictment will be filed, contributing to this region's reputation for rampant corruption.

"Dave Capp has done an excellent job in this county, but I think describing this area as a cesspool for rampant corruption is very strong," Petalas said. "I know that local editorial writers, cynical reporters and local bloggers would like to perceive Lake County in that light, but the unfortunate string of corruption cases is no bigger than it is in other large metropolitan areas."

"We just don't get to read about them because news from those areas is not readily available to us," he added. "However, what we do receive is television news from the Chicago Metro area. And we see on television news that corruption is all around us, and it does not have a party label. I do not think that one-party rule is a symptom of public corruption. That is an illusion created by the fact that this area's elected officials are primarily Democrats. In areas around the country where elected officials are primarily Republican, they, too, suffer from the same type of corruption in politics."

True, but most of the convicted public officials in Lake County have been affiliated with the Democratic Party, which has had a political stranglehold for several decades.

"There are many names that have been placed on the Lake County corruption list over the years. But some of those names are business people and some are Republicans who have used the political system to their advantage," Petalas said. "Larceny in someone's heart does not carry a party label."

Think quick: what names first come to mind when thinking of public corruption in this region? I asked this question to dozens of longtime voters, political insiders and casual observers. The list of their responses included familiar names such as Robert Pastrick, George Pabey, Thomas Philpot, Keith Soderquist and others from this era.

Petalas continued, "You also have to consider names from the past, like Rudy Bartolomei, George Chacharis, John Nicosia and others. In fact, the names from the past really were involved in some serious corruption cases. They were convicted for not only taking advantage of the system, but from profiting financially in an enormous way. Even after their stints in prison, they were well off. Those indicted recently, like Pabey, Philpot and Van Til, were choirboys compared to the names of old."

The crimes of these most recent offenders were indeed minor compared to those of elected officeholders from previous generations. Still, illegal *is* illegal.

"The money that exchanged hands was so minimal you wonder why these guys even bothered to do what they did," Petalas reasoned. "And most of them are now not only broken but also broke, financially flat broke."

For years, I have contended through my newspaper columns that part of the blame for generations of systemic public corruption should be placed on registered voters and the electorate, not only in their own municipality but also across Lake County. Not everyone agrees.

"I don't blame voters for not seeing or understanding the sophistication and the extent that public corruption has on our culture," said Thomas

Frank, an outspoken community activist from East Chicago. "I think public corruption is modeled alongside other forms of oppression, such as labor and racism. It goes back to the days of initially compromised social formations that industries created when they settled and organized workers here. Public corruption is not something of the past. Our judiciary system is subsumed by the fighting forces in our political economy. This is how and why great powerful wrongs go unaddressed."

Frank hosts what he describes as a "Toxic Tour"—an apt name for an eye-opening presentation featuring startling figures, graphic images and keen insights about northwest Indiana and its industrial legacy. For more than a century, we've worn that legacy as a badge of honor while conveniently ignoring its contaminated underbelly. We've willingly exchanged our collective health for comfortable homes and tons of pollution for steady paychecks.

"There is a reason why this region has so many marginalized communities and oppressed people," Frank said. "It's not by accident. And the fragmentation of civilized society is not by accident either. It's by purpose and for profit."

As always, with profit comes an opportunity for corruption.

"The real corruption in this region starts in the big industries. It always has," Frank said. "Our local leaders are only the front men."

Petalas believes more than 80 percent of Lake County voters base Election Day decisions solely on name recognition. "Unless it is a media-driven race, or a race for U.S. president, they have no clue who they are voting for. Most simply come out to do what they believe is their patriotic duty, and they simply vote for names that are recognizable."

Petalas has worked at polling places on Election Day for nearly four decades, casually chatting with voters each time as they enter or exit the voting site. He's routinely amazed, and quietly disheartened, when voters have no idea about their elected officials. Not only do they not know their representatives' names, but they also have no idea what they do for municipal government, he said.

"I have had people tell me they don't recognize me at all, but when I give them my name, they respond, 'Oh yeah, you're the guy on my tax bill.'" Petalas said.

Does this put voters at fault for our region's chronic corruption problems?

"Of course not," he replied. "Even if they vote for someone other than recognizable names, that doesn't mean that these new people will not be corrupt. By the same token, just because someone runs for office on a consistent basis, it does not make him or her corrupt either. New or old faces, the same party or one that is different, none of this is relevant. People's ethical boundaries have nothing do to with these factors. But you are never going to be able to stop public corruption completely any more than you will be able to stop crime in general."

Part II

Lake County, Indiana: Ground Zero for Hoosier Corruption

In 1962, our country's most famous and prominent lawyer at the time, U.S. attorney general Robert Kennedy, called Lake County, Indiana, the most corrupt county in the nation. Kennedy's quip has been repeated so many times in northwest Indiana that it has become legendary lore throughout the Calumet region. As a historical footnote, his harsh assessment also proved to be true.

In G. Gordon Liddy's autobiography, *Will*, the infamous attorney and chief operative from the Watergate scandal wrote, "The infamous Lake County, by reputation a hotbed of vice, corruption, organized crime, racial discord and a target of Soviet bloc espionage. I could hardly wait to get there." When he got there in 1957 for his first assignment with the FBI, he witnessed firsthand how organized crime brazenly ruled local government.

In June 1951, a grand jury completed the most exhaustive investigation in Lake County history into commercialized vice and gambling and the coalition between criminals and politicians. Over the course of six months, the six jurors heard more than three hundred witnesses, prompting them to indict more than twenty-five top county officials and hoodlums.

"During that time, more panderers, prostitutes, pimps, madams, perjurers, gamblers, hoodlums, racketeers, gangsters and their partners in crime—police officers, chiefs of police and mayors—paraded in and out of

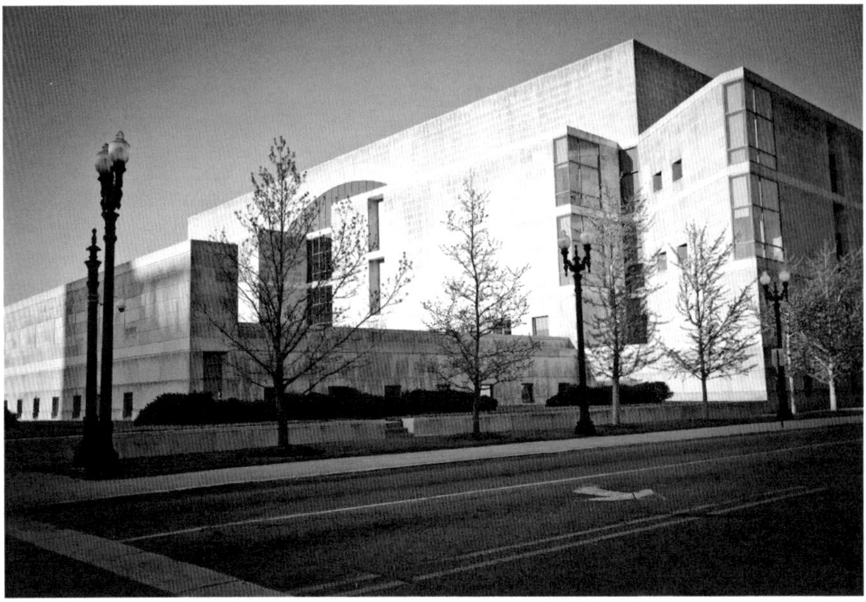

U.S. District Court Federal Courthouse, Hammond, Indiana, front view. *Courtesy of Joey Lax-Salinas.*

the criminal court building than in its previous twenty-five years," said Lake County prosecutor David Stanton.

As the old adage goes in Lake County, you don't have political constituents, you only have friends. And no matter what, above all else, and especially on Election Day, you take care of your friends. Period. End of campaign. Any campaign. Everybody else looked the other way with a wink and a nod, either out of political politeness, profound fear or blanketed apathy.

"When times were booming in Lake County, and unemployment levels were very low, nobody really cared that their government was a little crooked," said Hammond mayor Thomas McDermott Jr. "In fact, some residents speak of this chapter of Lake County's history with the same regard they speak of John Dillinger, who was a thief, a killer and, not coincidentally, has a museum in Lake County honoring him."

"Things changed, in my opinion, as times got harder in Lake County," he added. "As the steel mills—once a fixture of employment in Lake County—closed, the supporting businesses closed as well. Unemployment started rising, and people are now having a tougher time supporting their families. If people struggle, they are far less inclined to allow shenanigans from their elected officials."

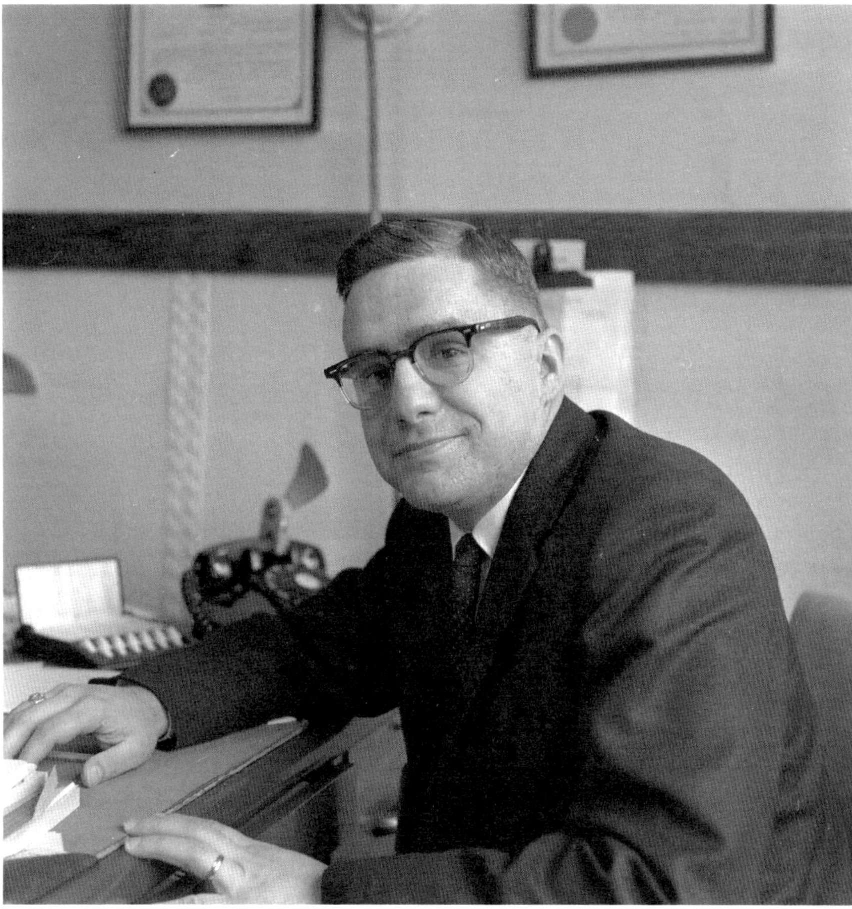

Former Lake County judge Orval Anderson, 1961. *Courtesy of Calumet Regional Archives.*

This zero-tolerance scenario seemed to hold true with the case of former Lake County surveyor George Van Til, whom I last wrote about in 2014. At that time, he was awaiting his sentence hearing for felony wire fraud after pleading guilty to using his surveyor's office staff, equipment and facilities for his reelection campaign. Although such practices have been commonplace in Lake County politics for decades—though still illegal—Van Til was exhaustively investigated, indicted and sentenced. Federal prosecutors made it a point to use Van Til as a high-profile whipping boy for every local public official who conducted such campaign practices. Countless officeholders did so, and many likely still do.

Van Til, who is in poor health, admitted his guilt at that time, hoping it would help his chances to avoid serious prison time, if any prison time at all. He hoped to be sentenced with a well-publicized slap on the wrist—house arrest and probation. Van Til correctly insisted he was a scapegoat for all the Lake County officeholders who have routinely used their offices—and taxpayer dollars—to boost their reelection efforts. His crime paled in comparison to more serious charges against other guilty pols. If his county office didn't use direct deposit paychecks for its employees, Van Til would not have been charged with wire fraud, he contended. Two of his former employees wore a wire for the feds and trapped Van Til into making incriminating statements, court documents show.

Van Til's many supporters rallied behind him despite public backlash from voters and residents. This is often where professional cronyism and personal relationships collide amid public corruption scandals.

"With this being the first time that he has come before any court, I am asking as sincerely as one knows how that you place him on probation and, if necessary, assign him to home detention, community service, or to pay a fine," wrote Indiana state representative Vernon Smith, who has known Van Til since their freshman year at Indiana University Northwest. Smith compared Van Til's crime to a similar crime committed by former state superintendent of education Tony Bennett, who received only a fine as punishment for similar crimes.

Instead, Van Til was sentenced to serve eighteen months at a correctional facility in Terre Haute, Indiana. It left him a broken man in many ways after being released in June 2016. His relatively short sentence will follow him to the grave. And he knows it.

For Lake County politicians who have lived the high life for so long, they are also sentenced to live in the shadow of their wrongdoing. All the explanations and rationalizations in the world cannot ultimately unlock this kind of emotional incarceration. For many of them, this will last much longer than any amount of time behind bars, serving as a psychological ball and chain until their deaths.

Since 2001, the U.S. Attorney's Office in this district has won convictions or guilty pleas in more than fifty public corruption cases against Lake County officials through a program dubbed Operation Restore Public Integrity. In the 1980s and early 1990s, another public corruption campaign dubbed "Operation Lights Out" targeted, in part, video gambling, a rising crime during that era. Raids were commonplace in Lake County bars and restaurants, with hundreds of machines confiscated. More than a dozen politicians and powerbrokers were indicted, revealing corruption at multiple levels of local government, yet again.

With that said, here is a laundry list of Lake County politicians who have been indicted, convicted and sentenced through the years. It's by no means a complete compilation or a detailed explanation of each one, which requires too many pages for a book of this size. But it gives you an idea of the depth and rampant corruption over the course of many decades.

An editorial in the *Northwest Indiana Sentinel* newspaper on April 9, 1964, summed up a timeless indictment against Lake County: "Lake County's reputation has been damaged by repeated betrayals of trust by public officials. This has had serious economic repercussions."

"Either way, the Lake County taxpayer and voter is getting gypped," stated an editorial in the *Times* newspaper on February 27, 1962.

Make no mistake, Lake County taxpayers and voters are still getting swindled.

RUDY BARTOLOMEI. In 1988, former Lake County sheriff Rudy Bartolomei disappeared, if only in name. That's when the lifelong Gary resident sold out his public official cronies to the federal government in exchange for a new name, new home and new lease on life. To this day, he still may be a card-carrying member of the federal witness protection program. He was a high-profile political powerhouse in Lake County, but he wanted one more feather in his cap after serving thirty-three years as a precinct committeeman in Gary, twenty-five years as a district captain and seven years as a county commissioner. When the county sheriff died of cancer in 1983, Bartolomei pounced on the vacancy.

Soon after he took the oath of office, if not many years earlier, he began betraying it.

Federal agents launched a lengthy investigation—dozens of witnesses over the course of ten months—while raiding his office, his questionable gun collection and his shady past in county politics. In 1985, a federal grand jury indicted Bartolomei and his wife for fifteen counts of extortion, racketeering, mail fraud, conspiracy and embezzlement of federal money over a six-year period. It involved countless kickbacks dating back to his days before becoming the top law enforcement official in the county.

"The charges against these people are politically motivated, and the government has no credible evidence to back them up," his attorney Max Cohen told reporters.

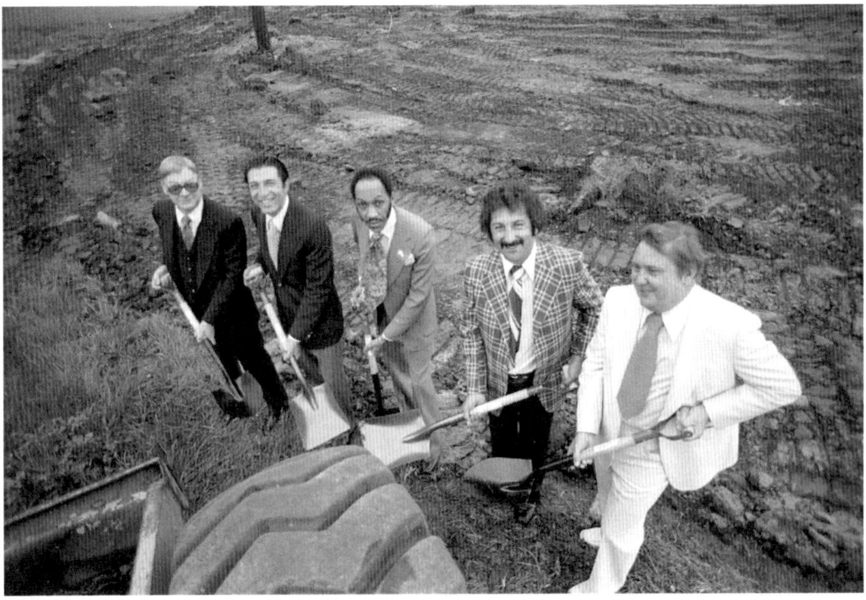

Rudy Bartolomei (*second from left*) at a groundbreaking ceremony for the new Lake County Animal Shelter. *Courtesy of Calumet Regional Archives.*

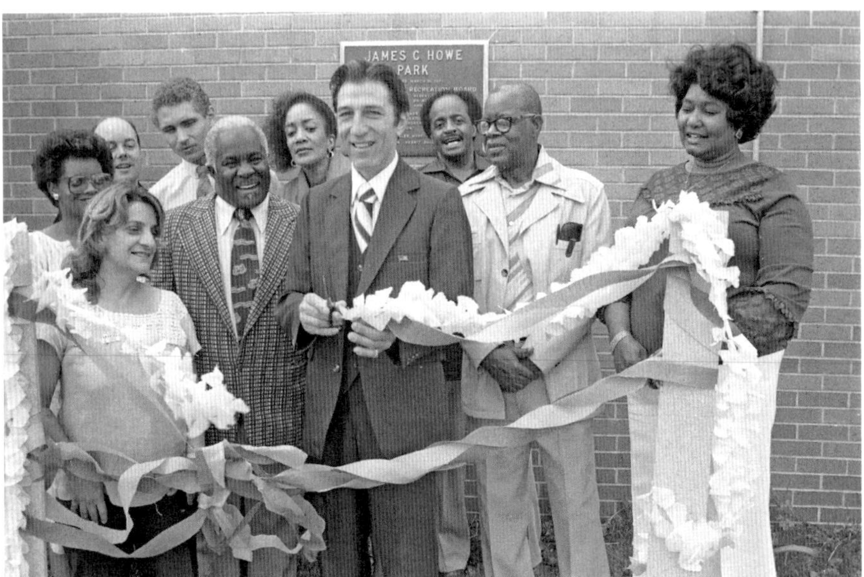

Rudy Bartolomei, opening ceremony for Howe Park Pavillion in Gary, 1980. *Courtesy of Calumet Regional Archives.*

That was not true, actually. The government had so much evidence that it offered Bartolomei a deal he couldn't refuse. If he would give damning evidence against several other public officials, he could disappear, if only by name. Bartolomei agreed to it.

In 1988, the man who used to be Rudy Bartolomei arrived at the federal courthouse in a monster mask to conceal his identity. He testified against his cohorts and fled town. He's been known to have secretly returned to the region for family-related events, but his permanent whereabouts are unknown. Whispered rumors of his death also have swirled around the region like a fallen leaf in an autumn gust. His infamous reputation, however, never left the region.

PETER BENJAMIN. Former Lake County auditor and assessor Peter Benjamin was charged and convicted of a lengthy list of federal crimes. In 2002, a federal grand jury indicted him on charges that he bribed a former Lake County Council president for lucrative county business, in addition to lying on federal tax forms to cover up payments to prostitutes and forging signatures of his wife and her grandparents.

Benjamin served as Lake County assessor from 1987 to 1994 and as county auditor from 1999 to 2002. He was forced to give up his law license after his conviction, costing him also a once lucrative law practice, a once happy marriage and a once bright future as a county Democratic leader.

After being accused of multiple charges, including bribery, money laundering, bank fraud, mail fraud and witness tampering, Benjamin told media, "I think a resignation would have been viewed by many people as an admission of guilt."

In 2003, he was sentenced to a fifty-one-month prison term, which was later reduced to twenty-three months, with previous time served, for his help in a federal investigation.

ROBERT CANTRELL. Robert Cantrell, a former North Township supervisor, was convicted in 2008 for numerous crimes. These included providing health insurance for his adult children who weren't on the city's payroll and steering contracts to a substance abuse counseling center for money kickbacks, federal prosecutors say. Cantrell served five years for mail fraud, tax fraud and insurance fraud and has paid $68,000 in restitution for his crimes. At his sentencing hearing, Cantrell was unapologetic for stealing money and deceiving the community, according to news accounts. As of

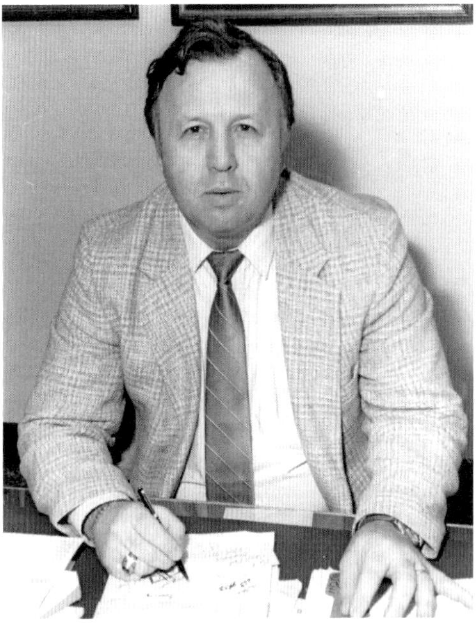

Robert Cantrell, East Chicago political operative. *Courtesy of East Chicago Public Library.*

this writing, the seventy-four-year-old political operative in Lake County continues to serve a three-year term of supervised release.

JAMES FIFE AND KAREN KRAHN-FIFE. In 2006, attorney James Fife and his wife, Karen Krahn-Fife, were sentenced to forty-seven months and twenty-four months, respectively, in federal prison for tax fraud. James Fife, an advisor to former East Chicago mayor Robert Pastrick, with his wife and former North Township trustee George Cvitkovich, schemed to form up to five phony corporations to avoid paying taxes, federal prosecutors alleged. Together, they scammed the city for more than $1 million from 1998 to 2001, court records show. In 2005, Cvitkovich was sentenced to three years in federal prison. At Fife's sentencing hearing, Judge James Moody told him, "This is an egregious crime. You should be ashamed of yourself. You did a disservice to your profession, the city of East Chicago, your family and friends. Shame on you."

WILLIE HARRIS, ROOSEVELT POWELL AND WILL SMITH. In 1999, the owners of a boarded-up building in the Miller section of Gary were interested in either selling or donating it. Will Smith, a Lake County councilman, notified Willie Harris, an attorney for the Gary Historical and Cultural Society, about the vacant building and its potential use to the organization. Harris's mother-in-law, Dharathula "Dolly" Millender, served as the society's longtime president. They agreed that the society would accept the abandoned grocery store as a donation. At that time, the building was appraised for $397,500, with $37,000 owed in taxes.

Roosevelt Powell, a tax collector for Lake County, entered the arrangement by convincing Jojuana Meeks, the executive director of the Gary Urban Enterprise Association (GUEA), to buy the vacant building for $200,000 in the name of the society. The property taxes then ballooned to $73,000. Harris and Powell concocted a scheme to lie about the condition of the building in order to get a reduced tax amount. Harris deposited the $200,000, writing a check to Smith for $75,000 and to Powell for $25,000.

However, no one notified the eighty-five-year-old Millender that not only did the society own a property that it couldn't afford but also her signature on a $200,000 check and the deed for the vacant Miller Building was forged. Plus, the historical society was stuck with the taxes owed on the building as well.

Powell, Smith and Harris were convicted of wire fraud, cheating Lake County government out of delinquent taxes and for cheating the society out of the proceeds through the complex scheme. Powell died in July 2016, at age seventy-four.

Metro Holovachka. After his return to this region from a brief stint at college and working for an out-of-district congressman, Metro Holovachka told reporters, "Lake County politics is no game for amateurs." Holovachka was, indeed, no amateur to the blood sport of local politics.

In 1948, he saw an opportunity to climb the ranks of Lake County politics as a prosecuting attorney. He campaigned to be the proverbial shining knight on a white horse to rescue the county from itself. He campaigned to take down a large gambling establishment dubbed the "Big House" in East Chicago. He campaigned to finally take down local crime leaders who kept giving Lake County a black eye in the national spotlight.

Nevertheless, on his first day in office, Holovachka tossed out most of the major indictments he had helped his predecessor, David P. Stanton, obtain. Citing "insufficient evidence," Holovachka also freed eight public officials from federal charges, setting the tone for his reign from 1953 to 1959. While serving as county prosecutor, he routinely used his office to "support and protect gambling and vice interests in Lake County," according to federal prosecutors.

Holovachka's dirty dealings in Lake County eventually caught the attention of U.S. attorney general Robert F. Kennedy and the U.S. Senate Rackets Committee. In 1963, Holovachka was sent to prison, charged with illegally dealing in Barrett bonds, as well as for tax evasion, supporting and protecting vice and gambling and making Lake County a sanctuary for syndicate hoodlums. He served only twenty-five months.

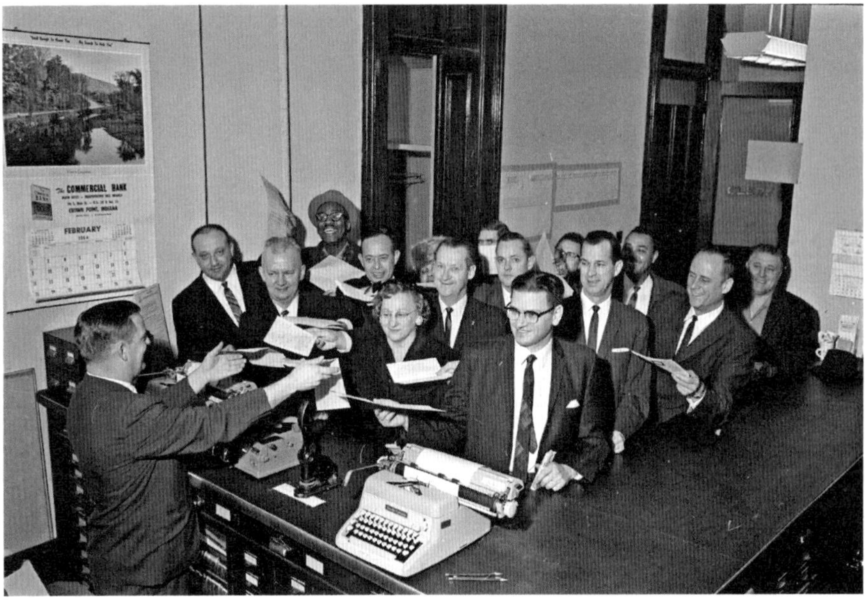

Lake County candidacy filing, including Vince Kirrin (*second from the left*), a politician who had influence over East Chicago and Lake County politics. *Courtesy of Calumet Regional Archives.*

Vincent J. Kirrin. In 1991, Lake County political powerbroker Vincent J. Kirrin, sixty-five, was convicted of conspiracy and mail fraud. Charges against the well-connected East Chicago native linked him to Midwest Building Services Incorporated, the company Lake County commissioners selected to clean the county government center in Crown Point, which cost $164,320 in 1985 and $276,144 in 1986. Kirrin, the feds alleged, was the true owner of Midwest Building Services, although the company listed Joseph Macko of East Chicago at its president, director, incorporator and sole shareholder. As Assistant U.S. Attorney David Capp said at the time, "Joe Macko's name was rented for $200 a month by Vince Kirrin." Kirrin was sentenced to three years in federal prison. He died in 1998.

Benjamin Lesniak Jr. Benjamin Lesniak Jr., a former East Chicago political figure turned government informant, went into hiding in 1975 during the government's probe of allegations into kickbacks to East Chicago city officials.

Michael L. Mokol Sr. In 1990, former Lake County police chief and Merrillville town councilman Michael L. Mokol Sr. was convicted of federal racketeering and illegal gambling charges for accepting bribes to provide police protection for illegal gambling. He served under the aforementioned Rudy Bartolomei and was sentenced to twenty years in prison. He died in 2007.

Thomas Philpot. In 2012, former Lake County clerk and coroner Thomas Philpot was sentenced to eighteen months in federal prison for stealing thousands of dollars in public child support incentive funds. The counts against him included theft and mail fraud.

Philpot held a college degree in podiatry and was also an attorney. He lost both licenses, as well as the privilege of serving in public office. According to senior U.S. District Court judge James Moody, Philpot's crimes were based on "arrogance, greed and a warped sense of entitlement."

The same can be said for most every Lake County official, both elected and appointed, who is guilty of public corruption. In one of his court motions, Philpot asked the judge to move his federal trial from Indiana to Illinois to avoid the "corrupted" jury pool here. His amusing list of "alarming insinuations" to bolster his request included this alleged name-calling: "Leech, fecal matter, a nugget that should be 'flushed,' an animal, a scumbag, a rapist, a thief, a man who steals from children, a liar, the former Illinois Governor Blagojevich, a depraved gadget and a shyster."

"Philpot is a name well known and associated with corruption. In reality, he has only been a very, very minor player in the whole scheme of things," said Marie Eisenstein, associate professor of political science at Indiana University Northwest in Gary.

As of this writing, multiple political insiders have recently told me about an ongoing federal investigation into yet another high-ranking Lake County public official, who I'm not allowed to name for obvious reasons. Will another indictment be coming from the feds' pipeline after this book gets published? I wouldn't be surprised. Would you?

5

East Chicago

"Last City Machine in America"

Until recently, East Chicago had been the de facto county seat of Lake County. This is mostly due to its once massive industrial tax base, allowing it to maintain an oversized government payroll, complete with patronage positions, meaning it could raise ungodly amounts of political

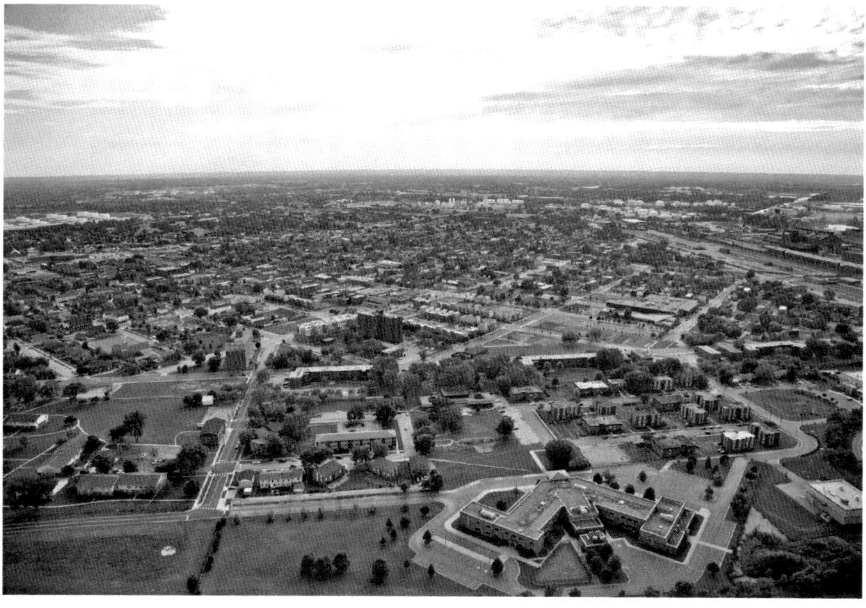

Aerial view of downtown East Chicago, Indiana. *Courtesy of Joey Lax-Salinas.*

money while delivering huge chunks of dependable voters. For the record, these were always voters who would punch the straight Democratic ticket no matter whose name was on the ballot, no questions asked. This allowed the city's leaders to punch above their weight, so to speak, not only locally but also downstate in Indianapolis and across the country.

"Everything that happens in Lake County has almost always led back to East Chicago," said veteran defense attorney Thomas Vanes.

In 1989, a now-collectible edition of *U.S. News & World Report* labeled East Chicago "the last city machine in America." Almost instantly, city officials proudly sported the derogatory moniker like a shiny new Cadillac.

"East Chicago has always been a very political community since Day One, as long as I've lived here," former East Chicago mayor Robert Pastrick said in a 1999 *Indiana Business* magazine story. "I guess it's an ethnic virtue, actually. As we came over, we had to depend so much on getting a job. Knowing someone, having some influence. And, of course, governance expected favors in return from those that they helped."

Pastrick served as political high priest in an ungodly municipality filled with Democrat disciples. He ruled with steely arrogance for more than three decades in office, inspiring a documentary, *The King of Steeltown: Hardball Politics in the Heartland.*

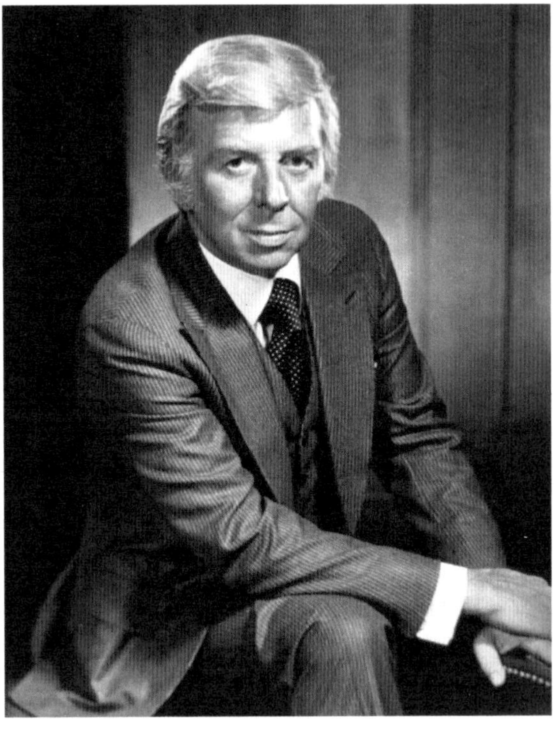

Former East Chicago mayor Robert Pastrick. *Courtesy of East Chicago Public Library.*

"In the past seventy-five years, there is no one in this region with as much notoriety as Pastrick," said Marie Eisenstein. "Pastrick is symbolic of a much more widespread and pernicious problem."

In 2004, Indiana attorney general Steve Carter helped draft a civil racketeering lawsuit against Pastrick, the first of its kind, claiming that he and two dozen codefendants operated the city as a criminal enterprise. Pastrick's dirty fingerprints were all over the city, Carter charged. Decades later, Pastrick's prints have yet to be rubbed clean from the city machine, even in its state of disrepair, his critics claim.

"Many of Pastrick's associates went to prison because of him," said Kim Krull, a retired chairwoman of the Republican Party in Lake County. "Associates like Babe Lopez and Jay Given probably died because of it. There are so many people that are still connected to that criminal enterprise."

None of those people would testify publicly against Pastrick, who never served any jail time for his alleged role. As one investigator told me, "No one would talk to us about Pastrick when his name came up. Even their body language changed. They just clammed up."

Pastrick, nonetheless, was found liable for $108 million in damages. He was targeted in the landmark civil racketeering case involving the so-called "sidewalks for votes" scandal in 1999. Federal agents, however, called this the "concrete" case, because tons of concrete were used to illegally garner votes.

"It was an obnoxious amount of concrete and money," said one federal investigator.

The scandal took place throughout the entire city, organized through Democratic precinct committeemen and a few city council members, most of whom were loyal to Pastrick. They literally went door to door buying support for Pastrick in exchange for new sidewalks, backyard patios, long driveways, in-ground swimming pools, even new roofs and other property amenities. Some particular concrete jobs cost taxpayers up to $130,000.

"God only knows what else may have been done inside those homes," said Augusto "Gus" Flores, former East Chicago police chief.

"On Election Day in May 1999, Bob Stiglich and I spent most of the day riding throughout the city, checking the polling places," Flores recalled. "I'll never forget what Stig told me at 1:00 p.m. that day: 'Gus, we've been buried in concrete.' Sadly, he was right."

Pastrick, however, would lose his office in 2004 to former police chief George Pabey, who became the first Hispanic mayor of the city. He campaigned to finally clean up the city after decades of crime and corruption, starting with city hall. But in 2010, he was indicted and later convicted for using city funds and labor to renovate a home he purchased in the Miller section of Gary. He was sold out by his former city supervisor Jose Camacho, who received a lesser sentence.

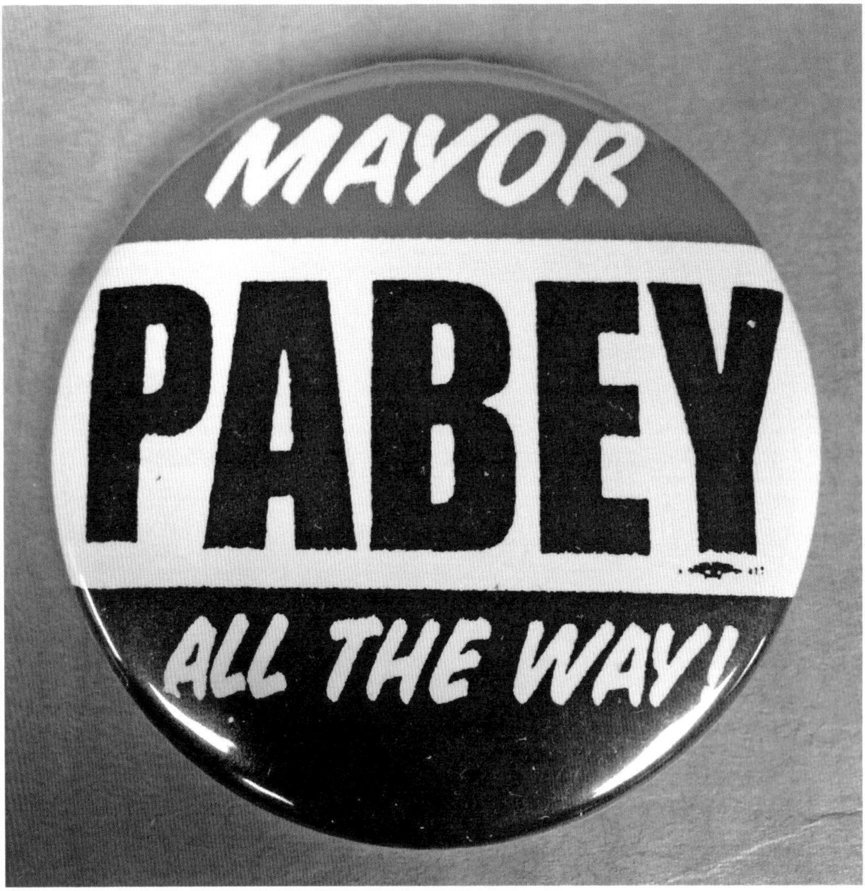

Campaign button for former East Chicago mayor George Pabey. *Courtesy of East Chicago Public Library.*

In a statement before his conviction, Pabey wrote, "I look forward to the opportunity along with my attorneys to my day in court and the chance to clear my name of these false allegations. Until that time, I will abide by the advice of my attorneys and not offer any additional public statement until given the opportunity in court."

Pabey was sentenced to five years in prison and ordered to pay a $60,000 fine. "Mr. Pabey focused his greed on a city that was a perennial target for corruption," U.S. district judge James Moody told the courtroom.

"I always felt that Pabey's administration couldn't adhere to the rules of plausible deniability," said Thomas Frank, a watchdog activist from East Chicago. "They were recklessly exposing their private backers to too many

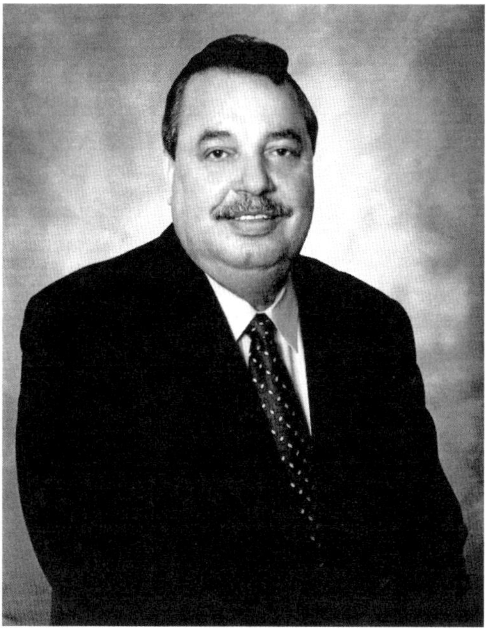

Former East Chicago mayor George Pabey. *Courtesy of East Chicago Public Library.*

potential dangers. I found it interesting how the [feds] were able to prosecute him on charges that isolate the corruption to his own private behavior, not the activities of the public-private partnerships that industry dictated."

Gus Flores came with his family to this country at the age of six, knowing only one word of English, "bread." His large family was poor, emigrating from the rural mountains of Puerto Rico with a hunger for the American dream. Like thousands of other immigrants to our smokestack skyline, Flores's father chose East Chicago to work at a steel mill. The family of eight arrived in 1950 with only hungry mouths and high expectations of America the Beautiful.

His family lived next to a notorious tavern called El Gato Negro (The Black Cat), a common site of criminal activity. One day, he watched two drunken men get into a fight with knives. The police arrived and cleared the scene. The situation carved another promise into the young, impressionable boy: someday he would be a police officer.

After dropping out of high school at age seventeen, in defiance to being unfairly cut from the basketball team, Flores joined the army. Basic training at Fort Knox, Kentucky, led him to Germany, assigned to the Third Medical Battalion of the Third Infantry Division. He arrived a boy. He left a man.

Flores returned to East Chicago determined to be a cop in his hometown. It didn't come easy. As you would suspect in that infamous city, you had to know someone who knew someone. A half century later, not much has changed there. Flores was the first Puerto Rican detective sergeant in the city's police department and, in 1985, possibly the first Puerto Rican police chief in the mainland United States. Along the way, he earned a GED and a college degree in criminal justice.

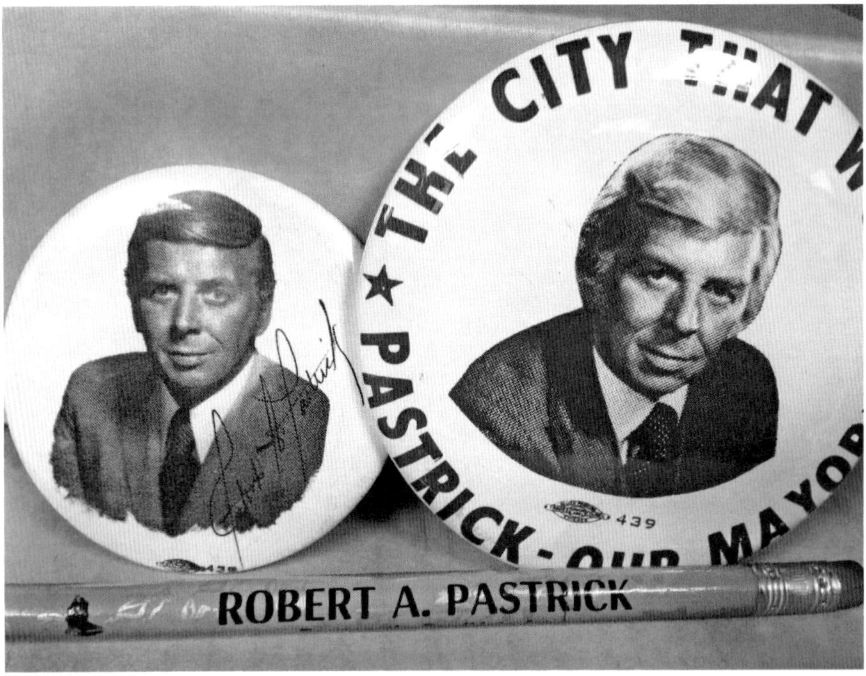

Campaign materials for former East Chicago mayor Robert Pastrick. *Courtesy of East Chicago Public Library.*

"I have to believe that the corruption that existed for so long contributed heavily to our city's downfall," said Flores, who still lives in East Chicago with his wife, Roberta. "It wasn't just the decline of the steel industry as past politicians will have you believe."

Flores witnessed a "change in the psyche" of East Chicago employees who were everyday, hardworking people before they were elected to public office.

"I don't know if it's the sense of power or the importance that changes them to the point that they compromised all their beliefs and good sense in order to get reelected," Flores said. "Whatever it took. I still don't believe that they ran for public office with the intent of becoming corrupt. I honestly believe that Bob Pastrick and George Pabey really did love the city of East Chicago. And, like Pastrick, George could have been mayor for life. I think the power and prestige of the office got the best of them, and they couldn't resist the temptations inherent in the position."

Like most every longtime East Chicago resident, Flores was familiar with the "Big House," a huge Las Vegas–style gambling operation located in the harbor section of the city. He remembers when his family first arrived there from Puerto Rico, they watched a parade of long, high-priced black cars, mostly Lincolns and Cadillacs, parked in that area near their home.

"The Chicago outfit that ran it hired East Chicago police officers to escort money couriers and big winners back to Chicago," Flores said. "I'm assuming that the outfit must have dumped a lot of money into politicians' pockets in order for the Big House to have survived for so long. And, they also supported other money-making interests as well, like prostitution and illegal booze."

Without question, the Big House was the most notorious gambling casino in Lake County history. Located at 3326 Michigan Avenue, it served as a workingman's Monte Carlo, if you will. Its operators, the late Warren "Sonny" Sheetz and William J. "Peck" Gardner, amassed small fortunes from the weekly paychecks of workingmen who habitually entered the shabby-looking two-story black building. After first being screened by the syndicate's muscle men outside the door, gamblers were free to lose their life savings inside the swanky venue.

It was once estimated to have earned each of its owners $2.5 million a year, thanks to Sheetz, who got his early training under Al Capone's mob during the Prohibition days. The Big House reached its highest point (or lowest point, depending on your point of view) in the late 1940s, reportedly

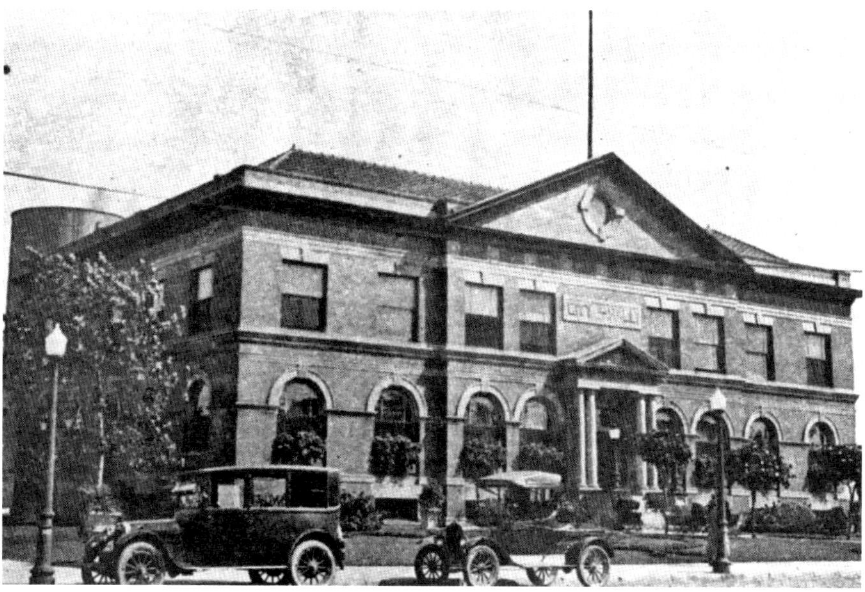

East Chicago City Hall, after the turn of the twentieth century. *Courtesy of East Chicago Public Library.*

becoming the largest gambling operation in Indiana, except for one in downstate French Lick.

According to the *Northwest Indiana Sentinel* newspaper, after the Big House got closed down, Gardner sold his upscale home at 9311 Lake Shore Drive in the Miller section of Gary and fled for Sarasota, Florida. He and Sheetz remained out of town when they were indicted by a Lake County grand jury. Also indicted were East Chicago mayor Frank Migas and other city officials. Sheetz later moved back to his Ivy Street residence in East Chicago to live out the rest of his days as a distinguished gentleman of means, the newspaper stated. He died in 1960 at the age of seventy-seven. Gardner died in 1954 at the age of eighty-five.

Only in East Chicago could a public official get reelected and receive a paycheck while behind bars for drug and murder charges. Yet this is exactly the stranger-than-fiction case of Robert "Coop" Battle, a Democrat representing the city's Third District. Although he ran unopposed, 308 voters punched his name on the ballot.

In September 2015, Battle was arrested in Porter County for possession of marijuana and more than $100,000. While that charge crept through the courts, Battle was arrested again in October 2015, for the fatal shooting of an East Chicago resident. Battle has pleaded not guilty and claimed self-defense in the shooting incident.

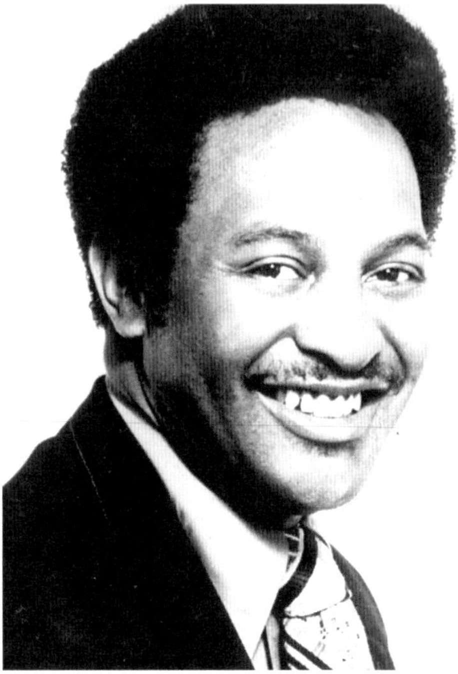

East Chicago public official N. Atterson Spann. *Courtesy of East Chicago Public Library.*

Due to reams of bureaucratic red tape and confounding legal loopholes, city officials struggled to force his resignation. The notion of allowing Battle to attend city council meetings electronically were even considered. Finally, after months of frustrating negotiations and researching of antiquated laws, Battle was unanimously voted out in May 2016.

Marla Spann can't escape her last name.

Born and raised in East Chicago, she's too often been judged by the actions of her uncle, Noah Atterson Spann. In 1988, the former county commissioner pleaded guilty to racketeering conspiracy and accepting tens of thousands of dollars in bribes arising from contracts to clean the county government center in Crown Point. He was sentenced to twenty years in prison, but his family's sentence of shame has lingered longer.

"I never could be myself because of my last name," said Marla Spann, a 1985 graduate of East Chicago Roosevelt High School. "My dream in life was to change my name and move away. But I returned to East Chicago and I've been here for twenty-five years."

Regardless of the mayor in office, Spann is skeptical that her city will ever be cleansed of corruption. She works in the East Chicago Public Library, where she's never too far away from boxes of old newspaper clippings of her city's political infamy.

"If anyone remains here who is attached politically to someone with a shady past, it will continue," she said. "Politics is ruthless in general, but it's especially true in this city. It's the same corrupt game but a new generation of different players."

At one time, the municipality located in the northern end of Lake County was called the Twin City of East Chicago and Indiana Harbor. Almost

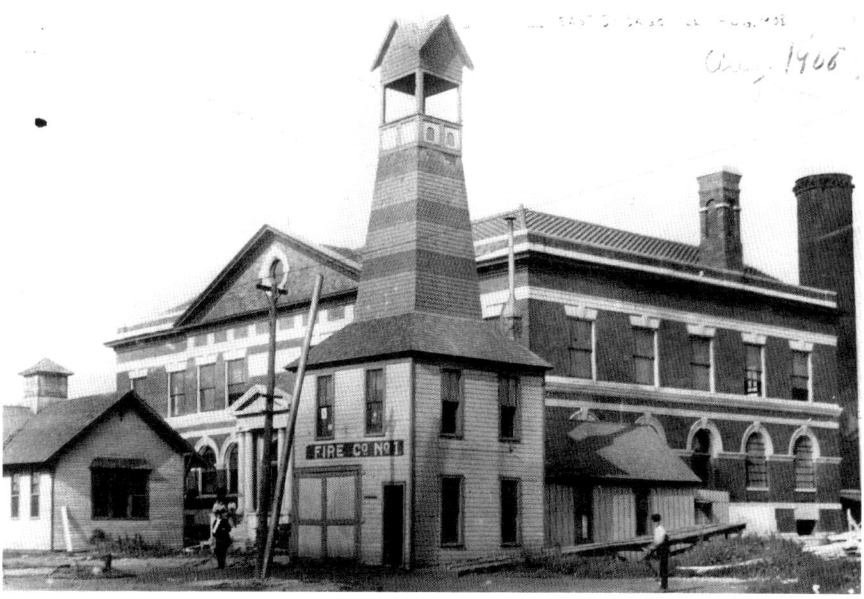

East Chicago City Hall, 1908. *Courtesy of East Chicago Public Library.*

from the very delivery of these identical twins, both were born with the deformities of graft, kickbacks and corruption. Pastrick and Pabey weren't the only mayors with shady histories. In 1979, former East Chicago mayor Dr. John B. Nicosia was convicted of obstructing justice for attempting to influence the testimony of the city's former sanitary district superintendent. His administration was accused of perjury, bribery and tax evasion during his reign from 1963 to 1971, but his sentence of eighteen months in prison was suspended due to his poor health.

Decades earlier, former East Chicago mayor Dr. Raleigh P. Hale was convicted for wrongdoing during Prohibition and sentenced to two years in prison.

As you see, the city's infamous reputation goes back much further than Pastrick's high-profile reign, the era of the Big House gambling joint or even the drunken days of Prohibition when East Chicago truly lived down to its big city name from across the state line.

On January 15, 1911, the front page of a Chicago newspaper screamed, "East Chicago Is the Most Graft-Ridden City in the United States!"

6
Gary

Corruption Goes Back Decades

On June 9, 1956, Gary mayor Peter Mandich wrote a commemorative letter to residents for the city's golden jubilee celebration that year. The multiday event was a grand affair for Gary's surging populace, roughly 160,000 strong, marking what may have been the zenith of the city's very existence.

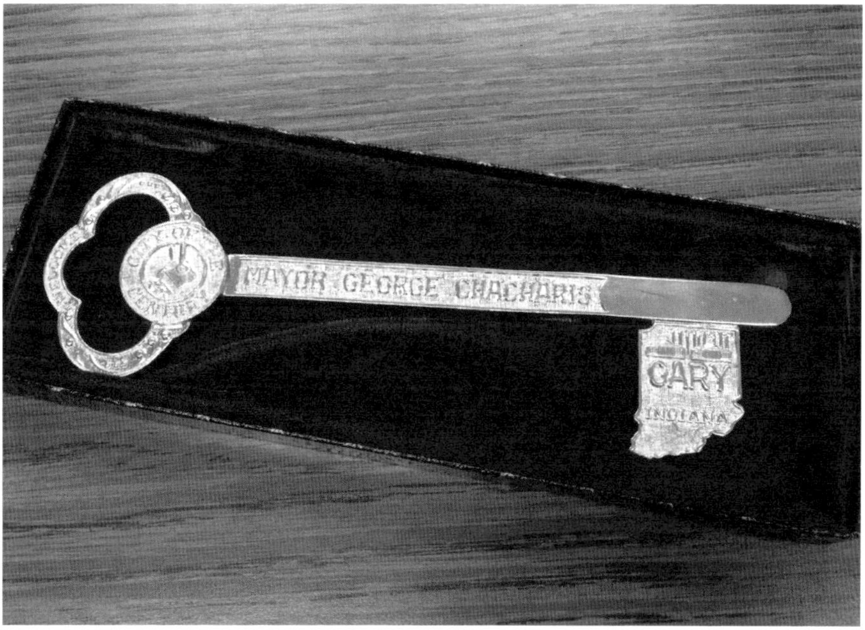

Opposite: Key to the city of Gary, golden jubilee celebration, 1956. *Courtesy of Jim Klodzen.*

"Having the distinction of being the first Mayor of Gary born in Gary," Mandich proudly wrote, "I take personal pride in having the privilege of serving our community during the Golden Jubilee. Gary is still a young city, still in the process of growing up."

The city's official historical souvenir program from that celebratory event dreamed of what Gary might look like fifty years in the future. In fact, page 73 featured a futuristic sketch titled, "Gary—2006 A.D.—The Magic City of Tomorrow," complete with sleek buildings, ultramodern designs and a bustling downtown area. Such an idealistic scenario seemed not only plausible at that time but also probable, if not inevitable. The city exuded hope and promise.

Behind that shining image, however, lurked a dark underbelly of public corruption from city hall on down to most every municipal office in some form or another. Bribes, kickbacks, collusion, conspiracy, backroom deals, graft, racketeering and tax evasion—these crimes were commonplace amid the hope and hoopla of the "Miracle City," as it was labeled during that era.

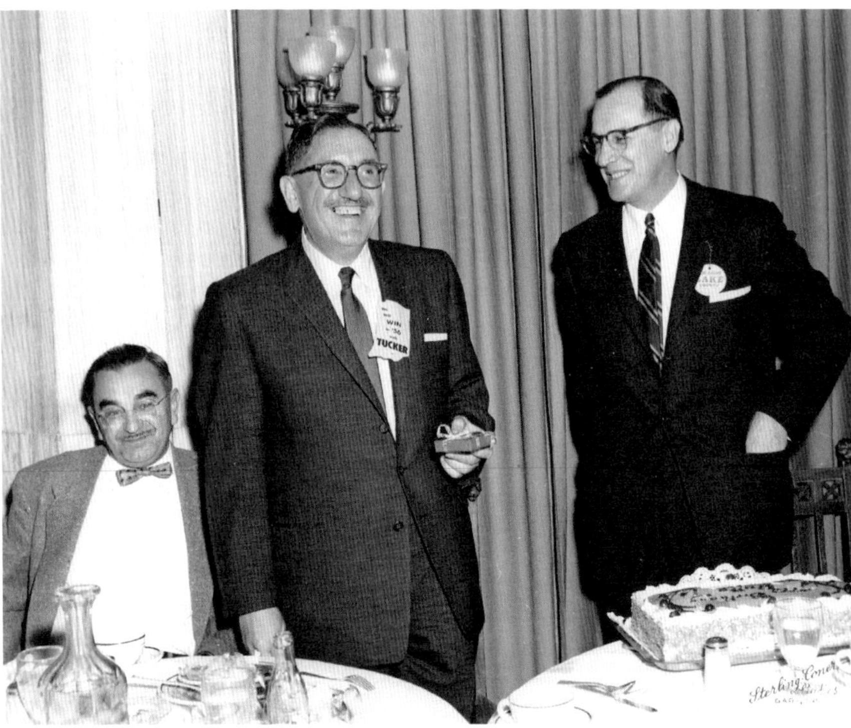

Former Lake County prosecutor Metro Holovachka, former Gary mayor George Chacharis and former Gary mayor Peter Mandich. *Courtesy of Calumet Regional Archives.*

"The heyday of public corruption in Gary was the 1950s and 1960s, with a great deal of gambling and prostitution," said Lake County historian Bruce Woods. "Gary had a very mixed population of many immigrants, perhaps making them susceptible to payoffs for voting."

A story in the long-defunct *Northwest Indiana Sentinel* newspaper, a short-lived sister paper of the *Gary Post-Tribune*, summed it up well: "Never has there been another era in Lake County history as bloody and savage as 'The Lawless Years' in Gary from 1930 to 1938."

During those infamous eras, it wasn't uncommon for precinct committeemen to drive around the city, pick up voters and drop them off at the polls on Election Day. "They would hand out money to vote the right ticket," Woods said.

Such voting day practices were nothing compared to everyday criminal acts under the guise of "city government." Still, as long as everyone in the city had a job, and money kept pouring in from U.S. Steel and related industries, there weren't many complaints—or convictions for that matter. This came

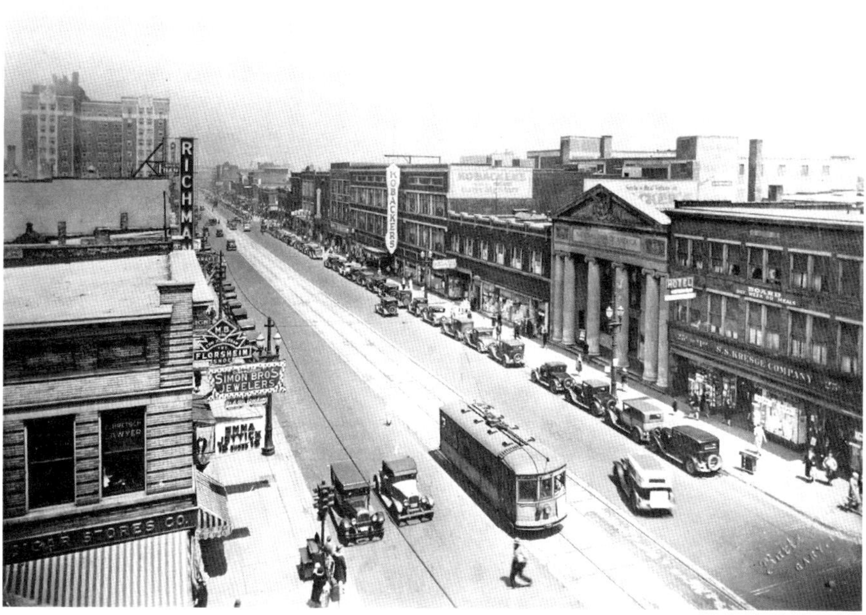

Broadway in downtown Gary, north of Seventh Avenue, 1928. *Courtesy of Calumet Regional Archives.*

to an abrupt halt in 1961, with the indictment of then Gary mayor George "Cha Cha" Chacharis for conspiracy to evade his income taxes. His old-time pal, close confidant and predecessor at city hall, Peter Mandich, who was Lake County sheriff at the time, was also indicted.

"Since there has been a great deal of speculation in the news media, I shall not try my case in the newspapers," Mandich said in a released statement. "These charges are absolutely unfounded and I stand by my record as a public official."

Prosecutors were convinced that Mandich, while serving as Gary mayor, "had received large amounts of graft payments," according to the indictment, but there was no concrete evidence that he didn't pay his federal income taxes on that dirty money.

After Chacharis later pleaded guilty to some of the charges against him, the charges against Mandich were eventually dropped. Still, his indictment surprised no one in Gary; the city's political history groomed both men for such behavior in public office. Chacharis pleaded guilty to the tax evasion charges, which often

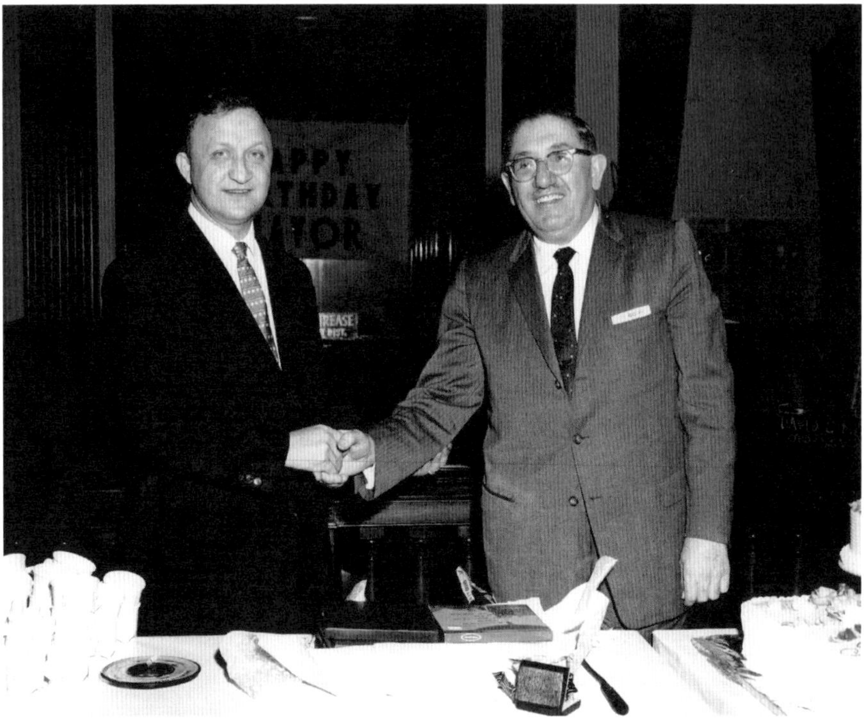

Former Gary mayors R.O. Johnson (*left*) and George Chacharis. *Courtesy of Calumet Regional Archives.*

served as the only criminal offense that federal prosecutors could pin on corrupt officials. If there is one mistake that racketeers should never make, it's not paying all of their income taxes. These officials were typically found guilty of the much lesser charge of refusing to share their swag with Uncle Sam. Too many Gary officeholders to count were pinched for this comparatively small-time crime, although they committed much larger crimes in their lives.

Chacharis was forced to resign as mayor and sentenced to serve nearly two years in a federal prison. Again, this surprised no one who knew him, except for those who were close to him and assumed he would somehow dodge those charges, too. At the time, these city leaders had an air of invincibility, which can still be felt while looking at old photos of them at public functions and political fundraisers. It's as if they felt impervious to any criminal charges against them, like bullets bouncing off Superman's chest. However, their arrogance also proved to be their kryptonite, as history teaches us.

"It is interesting to note that many officeholders did not get into trouble right away," Woods said. "I think there might be a sense of immunity that develops among them, perhaps even a sense of power. Even today, with all the emphasis on ethics in government and the history of indictments and sentencing, I suspect many believe it won't happen to them."

It did, though, eventually.

That dusty era may have been the heyday of corruption in Gary, but by no means was it the only time period that harbored—and hid—dirty dealings within city hall.

"So many names come to mind," Woods said. "Corruption was already beginning in the early 1920s with Gary mayor R.O. Johnson. Prior to that, Gary was described as a lawless town, similar to the Wild West."

In 1923, R.O. Johnson was convicted of conspiracy to violate the Volstead Act, though President Calvin Coolidge later granted him a pardon after his release. Johnson ran two more times for mayor, and not surprisingly in the city of Gary, both times were successful.

"Despite the mayor's friendly attitude toward U.S. Steel officials, they were upset by Johnson's indifference to the prevalence of prostitution and gambling in Gary," according to the Calumet Regional Archives at Indiana University Northwest.

This wink-and-nod attitude of approval continued for decades by various public officials throughout the growing city. With each criminal wave came attempts to curb its effects for future generations. In 1950, the Gary Crime Commission launched its first project, dubbed "The Microphone Speaks," a remarkable political document published for the masses.

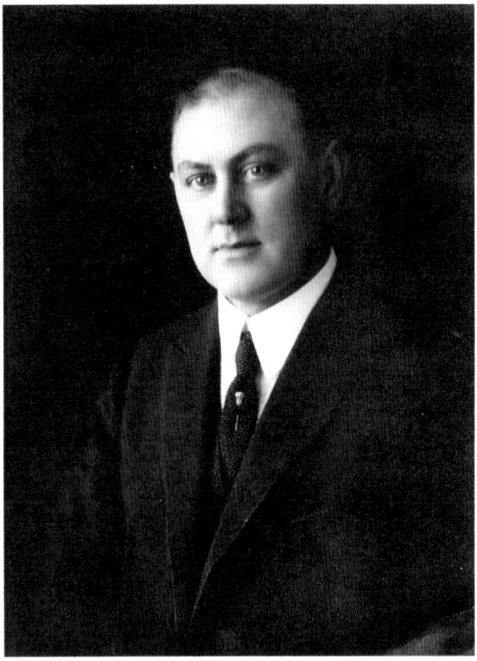

Former Gary mayor R.O. Johnson. *Courtesy of Calumet Regional Archives.*

During the course of its investigation, the commission determined that chief deputy prosecutor Blaz A. Lucas's office in Gary served as the nerve center for "fixing" cases in Gary City Court, according to the *Northwest Indiana Sentinel.*

Crime commission agents secretly installed a microphone in a light fixture inside Lucas's office. A wire from the microphone carried the conversations in the office to a tape recorder in a nearby attorney's office. For the first time, transcribed word-for-word conversations captured the innermost workings of a politico-crime syndicate.

The recordings revealed that Lucas engaged in several criminal activities, including:

- Ordering a Gary police detective to be an "enforcer" against two tavern owners whom Lucas said were politically "wrong"
- Fixing court cases and arranging to receive cash kickbacks for doing so
- Advising the operator of a house of prostitution on how to avoid arrest
- Forcing racketeers to contribute to the office's campaign fund

The surprising disclosures from "The Microphone Speaks" sparked public outrage throughout Gary and Lake County. It did so through more than 200,000 booklets printed by the Gary Crime Commission. Lucas quit as chief deputy prosecutor on the day after booklet was published, according to the *Sentinel* story. Despite such investigative campaigns, the corruption continued, though the faces changed.

George Chacharis, who was born in Thebes, Greece, arrived in this country with his family in 1918, first living in New York City and eventually

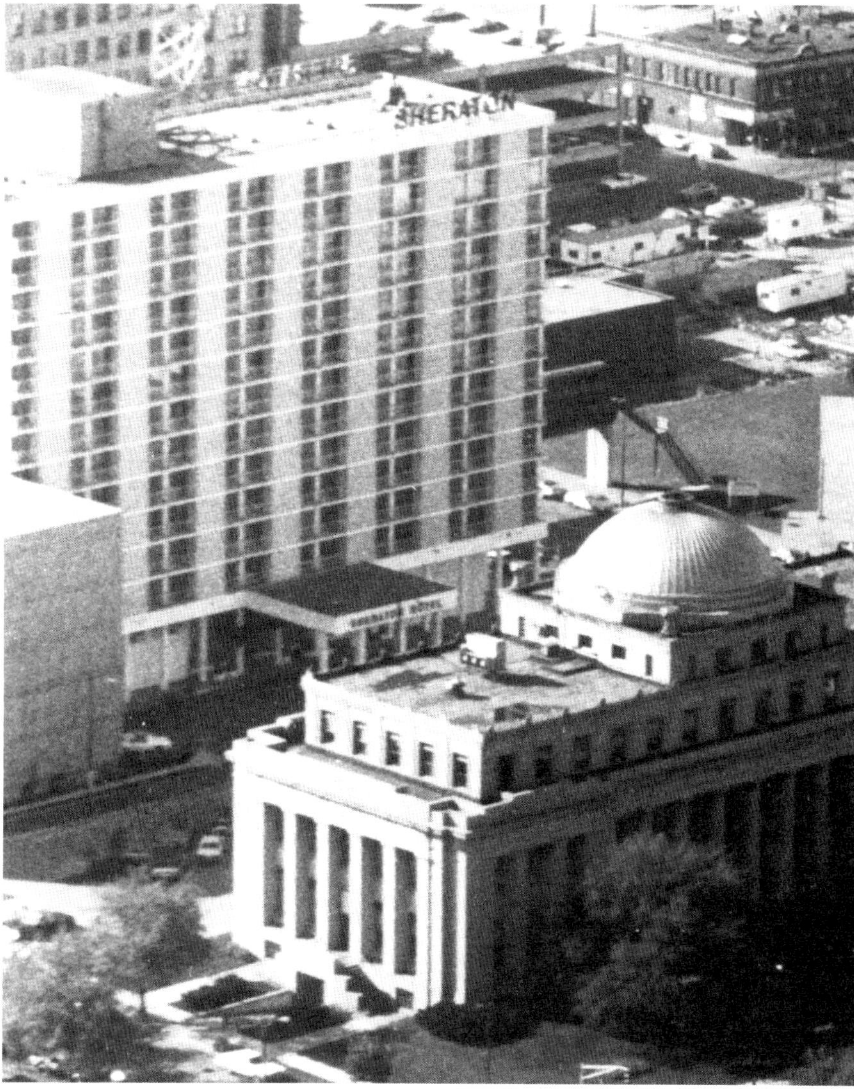

Gary City Hall, aerial view. *Courtesy of Calumet Regional Archives.*

moving to Gary. The Catholic altar boy later organized a social club with ethnic leanings named SAR, of which Peter Mandich was also a member. When Mandich became mayor in 1951, he appointed Chacharis as city controller. In 1958, Mandich resigned the city's top spot, opening the office door to Chacharis. Four years later, a grand jury indicted Chacharis and five other officials for conspiring to taking kickbacks from companies doing business with the city. He pleaded guilty in December 1962 and was sentenced to three years in prison.

Before his conviction and sentencing, however, Chacharis was the honored guest at a birthday dinner where roughly 1,500 guests paid twenty-five dollars a pop to provide a criminal defense fund, of sorts.

"Everyone called him 'Papa' and thought highly of him, even after he got into trouble," Woods explained. "This voter loyalty was often based on ethnic origins and, certainly, party affiliations."

According to a scathing editorial in the *Chicago Tribune* on February 23, 1962, "All the officials in these criminal proceedings are Democrats, which in Lake County means also that they have the blessing of the bosses of the steelworkers union. In Lake County, official misconduct seems to be taken so much for granted that public employees are forced to buy tickets to raise defense funds for officials."

Despite their criminal acts, many experts continue to insist that those corrupt bureaucrats still did a lot of good for the blossoming young city.

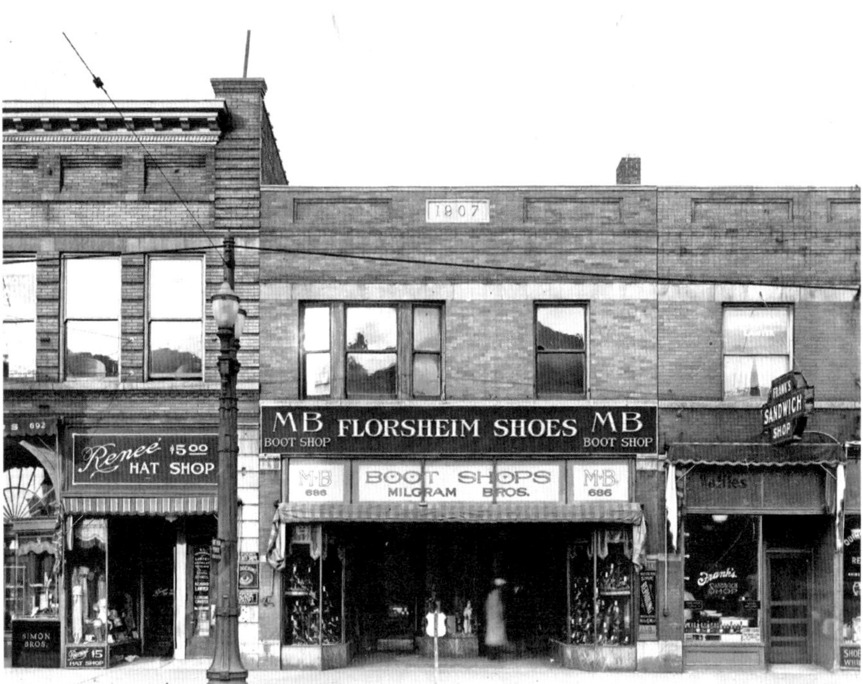

Downtown Gary streetscape, 1927. *Courtesy of Calumet Regional Archives.*

"The two Gary mayors who went to jail—R.O. Johnson and George Chacharis—were better for the city than most of their *honest* counterparts," said Calumet region historian James Lane.

Chacharis, who was paroled in December 1964, returned to Gary to work at the Calumet Township Assessor's office and, later, the Lake County Assessor's office. He died in 1983 of an inoperable brain tumor.

"The wake of the Chacharis conviction was probably the high water mark for attempts to reform local and, certainly, Gary politics," said Kendall Svengalis, a Gary native who authored the 2006 book *Gary, Indiana: A Centennial Celebration*.

As a teenager, Svengalis recalled taking a bus from Gary to Hammond to witness Chacharis's arraignment hearing at the U.S. District Courthouse. He missed the hearing, but he didn't miss all the cues about Gary politics during its heyday.

"What I remember chiefly was the way incumbent Democrat administrations used hiring practices to retain political power," he said. "City employees were not precluded from engaging in political activity in their off-duty hours, and they were expected to work in campaign organizations, serve as precinct committeemen or committeewomen and contribute to campaigns. Concerns about job security were sufficient to enforce compliance, and contributions. It was a built-in advantage to the party in power."

"This widening of the net from employees to their circles of friends gave Democrats a clear advantage over weaker and disparate Republican efforts," Svengalis said. "Democrat politicians spread the wealth around to earn support from local constituencies."

For example, the metal folding chairs at the Saints Constantine and Helen Greek Orthodox Church were donated by Chacharis, the city's first foreign-born mayor. Stamped on the underside of each chair was the phrase, "Courtesy of George Chacharis," Svengalis said.

"Church leaders didn't question from whence the funds had come," he wryly noted.

This dominance of local Democrats emboldened them to engage in corrupt practices such as soliciting bribes from contractors who wanted city business, which got Chacharis in trouble with federal prosecutors. The high cost of doing business in Gary was revealed when a New Jersey contractor, whose firm had won contracts totaling $9 million for two sections of the Indiana Toll Road through the Steel City, testified that he paid $110,350 to get a $5 permit to excavate sand needed for road fill.

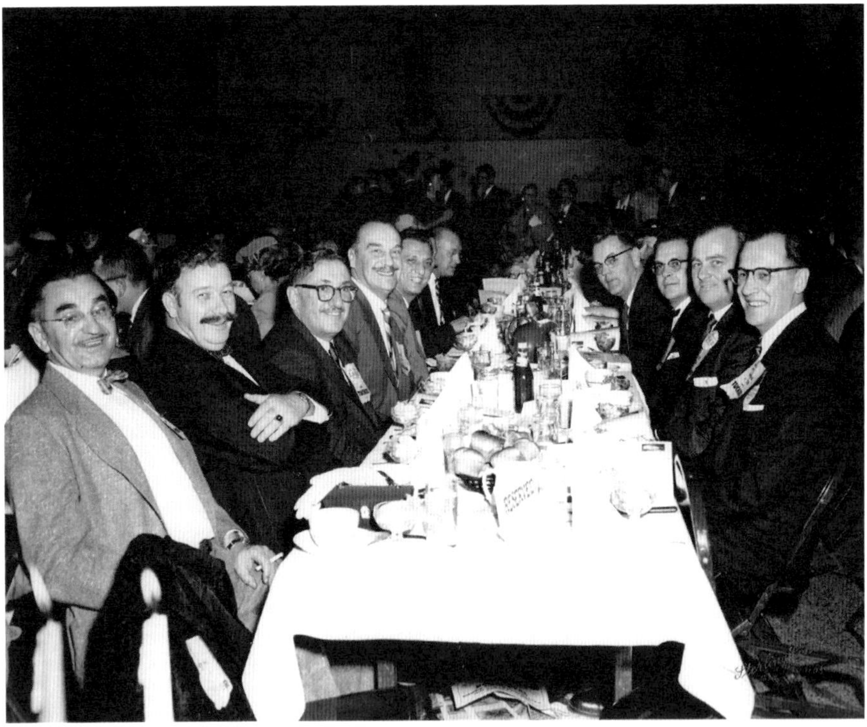

Former Lake County prosecutor Metro Holovachka (*far left*) and former Gary mayor George Chacharis (*third from left*) with cronies at a political dinner. *Courtesy of Calumet Regional Archives.*

"The *Post-Tribune* newspaper was filled with such stories in the early '60s," Svengalis said.

White flight, Svengalis reasoned, was far more than a racially fueled phenomenon in the city during the late 1960s and 1970s.

"It was a response to a corrupt environment where crime was tolerated by local authorities," he said. "I don't know how many times that people I've interviewed have said, 'Gary was a great place to grow up.' But that positive statement ignored the dark underbelly of criminal activity in Gary that was much related to its working-class demographics and its proximity to criminal activity in Chicago."

Svengalis agreed with the *Chicago Tribune* editorial from 1962 that the Democrats' lock on Gary electoral politics was cemented by the "incestuous link," as he described it, between the unions, chiefly U.S. Steelworkers, and the Democratic Party.

"Forced union membership, and the attendant dues, financed the party through thick and thin, regardless of revelations of public corruption," he

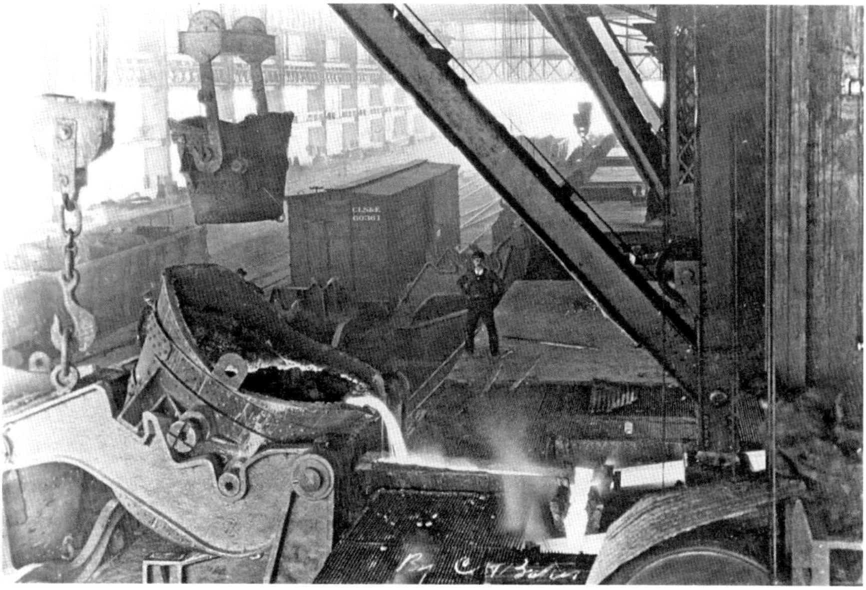

A U.S. Steel worker watches molten metal pouring at the Gary Works plant. *Courtesy of Calumet Regional Archives.*

said. "As long as Democrat politicians supported the union agenda, the unions could be counted on to return the favor."

His father, Frank Svengalis, who was politically astute but not politically active, resented the fact that his dues were used to underwrite the Democrat campaign efforts, Svengalis noted.

"I'm sure many other reform-minded steelworkers felt the same way as my father, but they were powerless to do much about the fact that a portion of their hard-earned wages went into Democrat campaign coffers," Svengalis said. "Most were too busy trying to make a living and scrape up enough to put their kids through college."

"While most supported the right to bargain collectively, they did not necessarily support what Democrat politicians were doing in, and to, Gary," he said. "It was a package, and you ended supporting the entire agenda of those in charge, including the corruption. Essentially, union leaders were overwhelmingly Democrats and they used dues from general membership to support their party. In my view, organized labor has a lot to answer for in its underwriting and tolerance of Gary, and Lake County, corruption."

In the fall of 1965, Svengalis left Gary for Purdue University. He didn't look back.

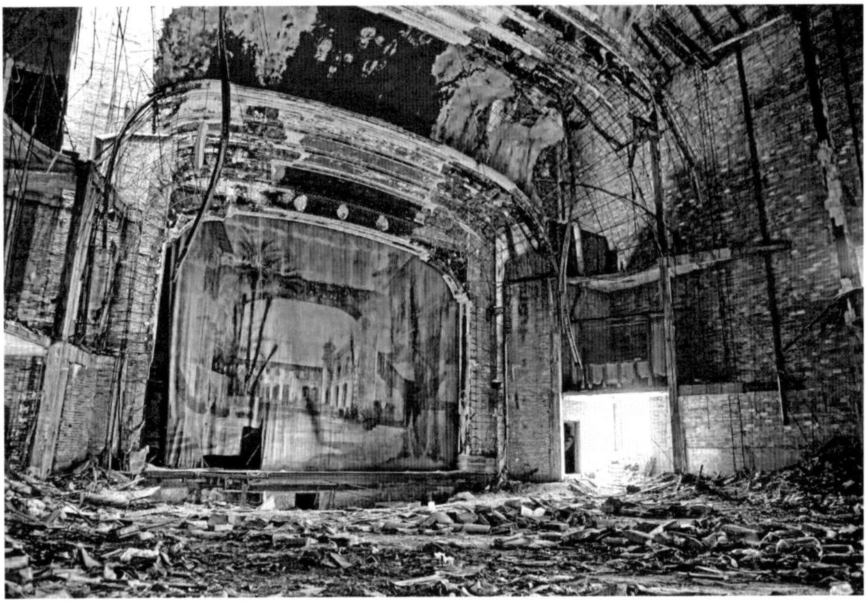

Palace Theater, Gary, Indiana. *Courtesy of Joey Lax-Salinas.*

"I left Gary politics behind," he said. "In retrospect, I look back on this as just one of the reasons why young people see no reason to stay or return to Gary, particularly after going to college and experiencing the world outside the narrow confines of corrupt politics and crime."

In retrospect, the city's chronic corruption problems either forced good residents to flee or flirted with others to return for personal gain. One of those residents in the latter category was Metro Holovachka, who, like Chacharis, was the son of immigrants.

Holovachka graduated from Gary's Froebel High School in 1927 and attended Purdue University, majoring in engineering. After two years there, he engineered a new career by working for a local congressman. He returned to Gary a new man under the "New Deal" attitude toward local government. Eventually, though, he got caught dealing from the bottom of the deck, politically speaking.

The alliance between politicians and criminals reached its peak of power from 1953 to 1959, an era that is commonly referred to as the "good old days" in Gary and Lake County's notorious history. Behind such idyllic remembrances of that seemingly innocent era is the fact that corruption flourished in the Calumet region. It's no coincidence that Holovachka served in public offices during that time span. The public found this out years later, after everything came out in an indictment by federal prosecutors.

In 1963, Holovachka was sent to prison, charged with illegally dealing in Barrett bonds, as well as for tax evasion, supporting and protecting vice and gambling and making Lake County a sanctuary for syndicate hoodlums, according to news accounts. He also aided in the development of a $15 million "pinball syndicate." Yes, a pinball machine syndicate illegally raked in millions of dollars over the course of many years.

Holovachka was later sentenced to three years in prison but served twenty-five months. (For more details on Holovachka, see the chapter on Lake County public corruption.)

"Special credit must be given to young Robert F. Kennedy, the Attorney General and brother of the President," stated an editorial in the *Times*.

"The public can take heart that Lake County politicos—of both parties—are undergoing close scrutiny by the federal investigators," stated an editorial in the *Sentinel*. "It will be a bright chapter in Lake County history if the house-cleaning goes from cellar to attic."

Since this scandalous era in the city, dozens of other Gary area officials have followed in the disgraced footsteps of their officeholder predecessors. The following is just a sampling from a lengthy laundry list of modern-day

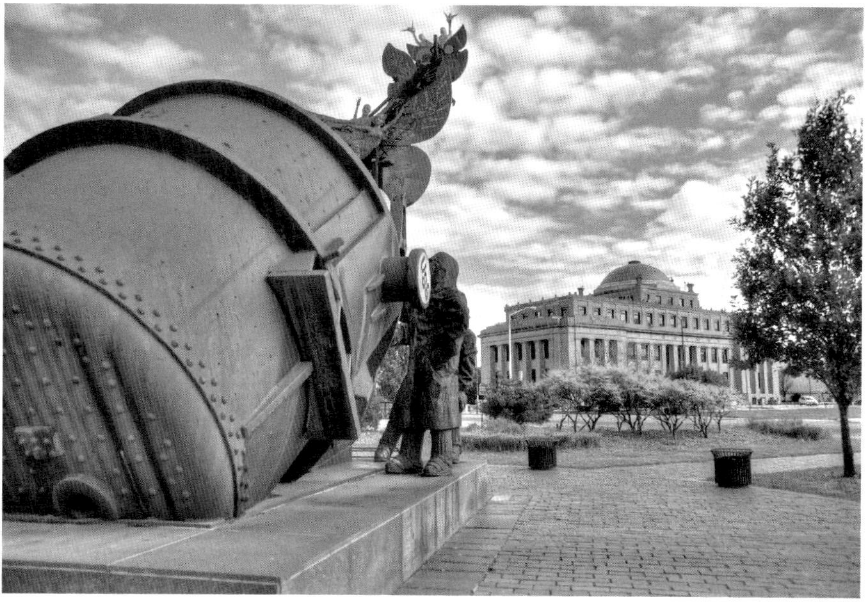

Downtown Gary, Indiana. *Courtesy of Joey Lax-Salinas.*

politicians who have also used public resources illegally for personal gain. It's by no means a thorough list, which would easily make this book twice its size.

Dozier Allen Jr. Despite thirty-plus years of noble public service, former Calumet Township trustee Dozier Allen Jr. was sentenced in April 2010 for mail fraud after being convicted with two of his deputies, Wanda Joshua and Ann Marie Karras. The discredited trustee also dipped into a separate fund earmarked for job development. A judge ordered Allen, seventy-nine at the time, to serve eighteen months in federal prison. Joshua was sentenced to fifteen months, and all three were ordered to split a $143,000 restitution bill for stealing public grant money intended for the poor.

Derrick Earls, Jojuana Meeks, Charmaine Pratchett and Johnnie Wright. Jojuana Meeks, former director of the Gary Urban Enterprise Association, was sentenced in 2007 to six years in federal prison for stealing more than $1 million from the nonprofit organization. Meeks pleaded guilty to the embezzlement, and she was ordered to pay $1.16 million in restitution in addition to $89,000 to the IRS for unpaid taxes. Charmaine Pratchett, who served as the former fiscal manager for GUEA, was convicted also and sentenced to seven years and three months. Former board members Derrick Earls and Johnnie Wright were convicted as well.

Mary Elgin. In December 2014, former Calumet Township trustee Mary Elgin was charged with several counts of felony fraud, including lying to the FBI during its investigation and manipulating political payments from government employees. The federal investigation revealed that she allegedly used employees to further her campaign by having them sell or purchase fundraising tickets while they were on the taxpayer's timecard. Elgin, who was seventy at that time, began serving in office in 2003 and was reelected to subsequent terms. Her trial is scheduled for early 2017.

Katie and Junifer Hall. How the mighty can fall is no clearer illustrated than through the story of former Gary city clerk Katie Hall and her daughter Junifer Hall. Katie Hall was a former state representative and the first African American woman from Indiana to serve in Congress. In 2002, a federal grand jury indicted the pair on charges of racketeering, mail fraud, conspiracy and extortion. Katie Hall hired her daughter as deputy clerk, and according to the U.S. Attorney's Office, the two "knowingly devised and participated in a scheme to defraud the city," while also employing another one of Hall's daughters, Jacqueline. According to prosecutors, Jacqueline Hall received paychecks and employee benefits, including medical coverage, but did not perform work for the city.

Several clerk's office employees alerted newspapers to problems in the office, prompting the FBI to get involved, along with the IRS and Indiana State Police. Katie Hall pleaded guilty, resigned from office and served probation and house arrest. Junifer Hall pleaded guilty to mail fraud and served sixteen months in federal prison. Katie Hall died in 2012, at age seventy-three.

Marilyn Krusas. Former Gary Common Council member Marilyn Krusas died in January 2016, less than a year after being released from federal prison. She pleaded guilty for failing to file tax returns for twenty years, serving one year and one day in prison. Krusas served on the Gary Council from 2000 to 2013, when she resigned after admitting her guilt in court. Federal prosecutors accused her of hiding $232,000 from an inheritance by writing checks of less than $10,000 to her sister to avoid legal reporting requirements. She was seventy-two.

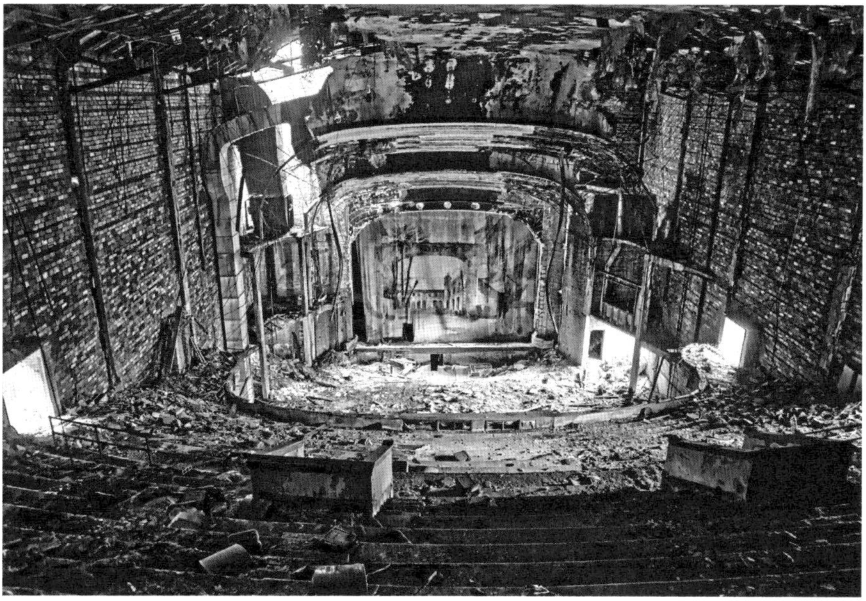

Palace Theater, Gary, Indiana. *Courtesy of Joey Lax-Salinas.*

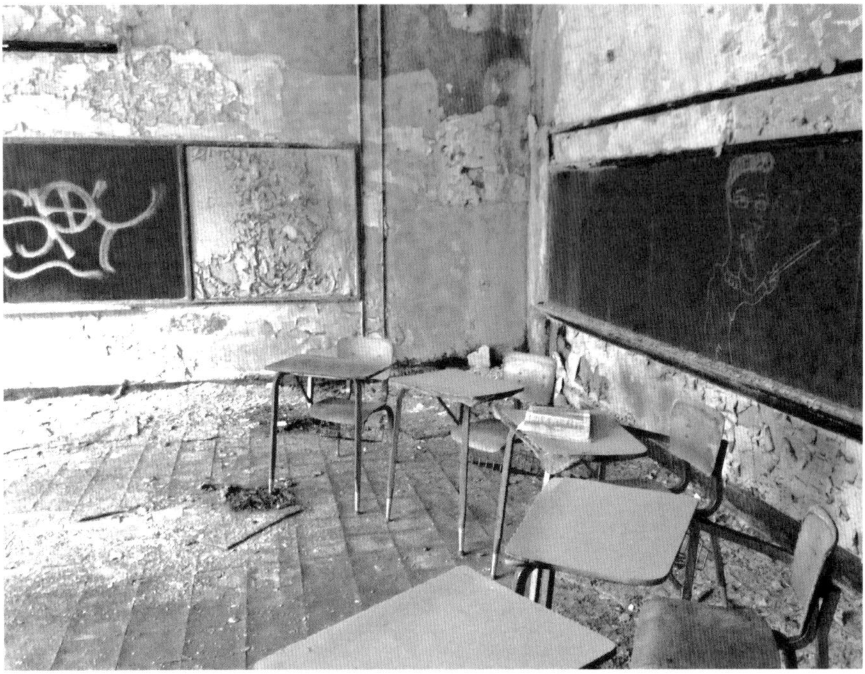

Emerson High School classroom after closure. *Author's collection.*

In 1956, during the city's golden jubilee celebration, no one could have imagined how many future city officials would be convicted of corruption over the course of the next fifty years. Those hopeful citizens never would have dreamed how off-base their pie-in-the-sky images would turn out to be in the so-called Miracle City, which would face white flight, racial hostility, economic downfall, political upheaval and troubled times for the city's 100th birthday and beyond. (For more details on this history lesson, see my previous book, *Lost Gary, Indiana*, published by The History Press.)

7

Lake Station

Modern-Day Corruption

Former Lake Station mayor Keith Soderquist could easily serve as the poster child for modern-day public corruption in northwest Indiana.

The former eight-year city councilman pleaded guilty to improperly and illegally using money from his reelection campaign, roughly $35,000, and

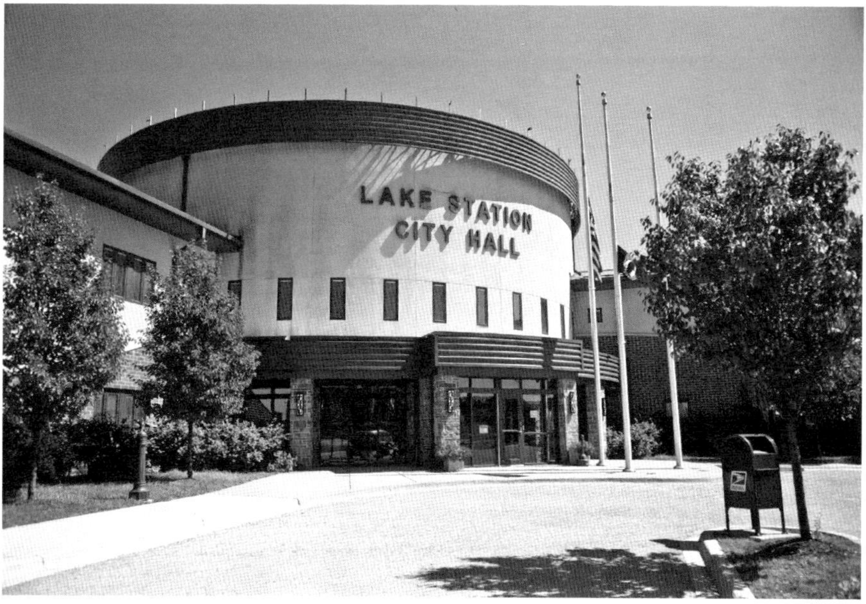

Lake Station City Hall. *Courtesy of Joey Lax-Salinas.*

from the city's food pantry, roughly $5,000. The stolen funds were then used to quench his appetite for gambling at a local casino, losing more than $100,000 at slot machines over a three-year period with his wife, Deborah, federal prosecutors say.

After deliberating only five hours after an eight-day trial, a U.S. District Court jury found Soderquist, forty-seven, and his wife, fifty-eight, guilty of conspiracy to commit wire fraud, seven counts of wire fraud and three counts of false filing. The couple, flanked by their attorneys inside the courtroom, did not say a word after the verdict was rendered.

"They both knew they were guilty," said Kim Frizzell, the city's administrative assistant and a longtime city employee. "He essentially cased the joint during his time as a city councilman, learned how to manipulate people and using his terms as a training ground for public corruption later in his career. He had an agenda from early on."

In 2014, Frizzell took the city council to task publicly for not looking into Soderquist's questionable actions involving the missing money; the actions of his his wife, who worked as his administrative assistant; and those of his stepdaughter Miranda Brakley, who had worked for the city as a court clerk.

"I can't believe what politics did to this city, along with a city council that just stood by and watched the entire thing unravel," said Frizzell, who started working for the city in 1988 as a municipal water department employee.

There's a contentious history between Soderquist and Frizzell. In 2012, Frizzell was wrongly laid off by Soderquist for six months, until city court judge Chris Anderson hired her to work as the clerk in his office. Soderquist tried blocking her hiring by Anderson, but Soderquist had no legal grounds to do so. Anderson earlier fired Brakley for stealing posted bond money in the court. Soderquist illegally and unsuccessfully tried to scrap the city court office in retaliation. Anderson ended up blowing the whistle on the Soderquists by contacting a former Lake Station police officer who was a U.S. marshal and who connected Anderson with federal agents.

"Something is wrong here," Anderson told federal authorities.

Anderson shared Brakley's computer with federal agents, and he returned it to city hall the next day. Around the same time, the Indiana State Board of Accounts paid a routine visit to city hall.

"It just so happened that when they were here, residents were here asking about their bond money," Anderson said.

"As soon as they opened that safe, everyone knew there was a serious problem here," Frizzell said.

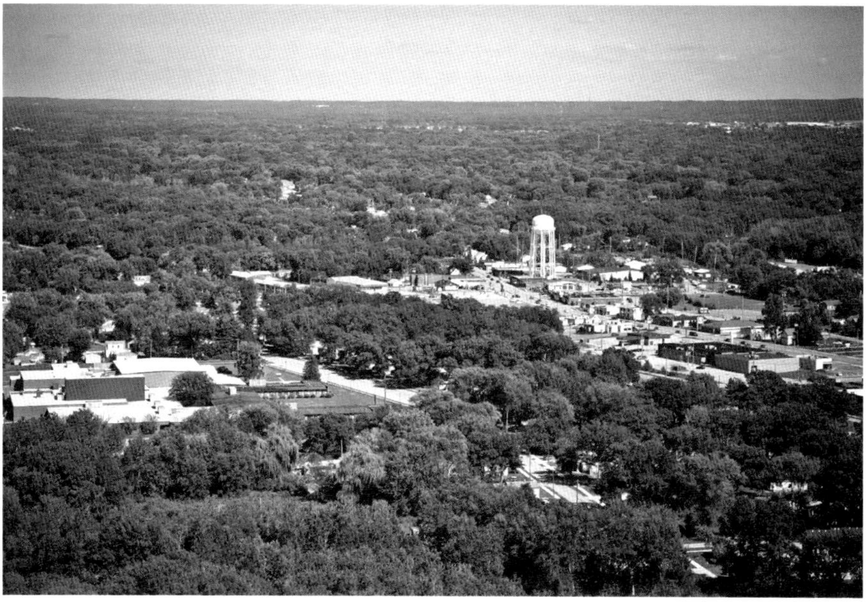

Aerial view of downtown Lake Station, Indiana. *Courtesy of Joey Lax-Salinas.*

Soderquist would later plead guilty to helping Brakley attempt to hide her crime of stealing $16,000 from city coffers. In a statement to U.S. magistrate judge Paul Cherry, Soderquist admitted his guilt from 2012 in helping to conceal his stepdaughter's crimes. He went as far as to arrange for a loan of $15,000 from a third-party source to help Brakley cobble together the missing funds.

"That money Soderquist gave his stepdaughter was all crisp bills, like from a bank, not from bond money, which could be in wrinkled bills and even coins," Anderson said.

Brakley pleaded guilty to one count of stealing from the city by embezzling deposit bond payments for her own use. According to the initial indictment, the feds' investigation was initiated after a State Board of Accounts audit disclosed missing funds that had been posted as bond money with the Lake Station City Court. The indictment also claimed that over a three-year period, the Soderquists withdrew funds from the bank account of the Committee to Elect Keith Soderquist.

"The three of them felt so arrogant and powerful that they assumed no one would ever catch them. And that they could get away with everything," Frizzell said. "Their crimes spread like a cancer in this city."

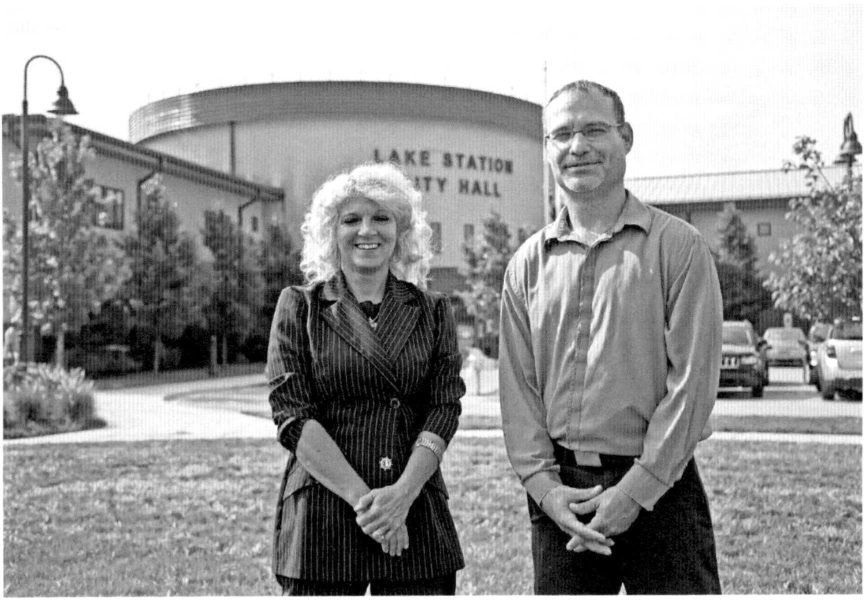

Lake Station mayor Chris Anderson and administrative assistant Kim Frizzell in front of city hall. *Courtesy of Joey Lax-Salinas.*

"And it's been tough to cure," added Anderson, a soft-spoken man with a serious attitude.

Anderson was later elected mayor, after Soderquist's indictment and conviction, taking office on January 1, 2016.

As Soderquist and his wife faced their sentencing in late September 2016, federal officials charged Soderquist with yet another crime. They revealed that he had set up a system of recording and listening to telephone calls within city hall. As mayor, he recorded approximately 425,000 calls between 2011 and 2015, even after being released on bond as his corruption cases were pending, according to a sentencing agreement.

According to court records, Soderquist listened to fourteen calls involving potential government witnesses at city hall and at least one call from Anderson's private office. For this added crime of violating a federal wiretapping statute, Soderquist faced an enhanced prison term of forty-two months.

The family's criminal actions were littered with complexities, as with most convicted public officeholders, but essentially, the feds caught them with their hands in the taxpayers' pockets. Their stolen money trail led in part to a gambling habit. In the indictments, U.S. attorney David Capp said

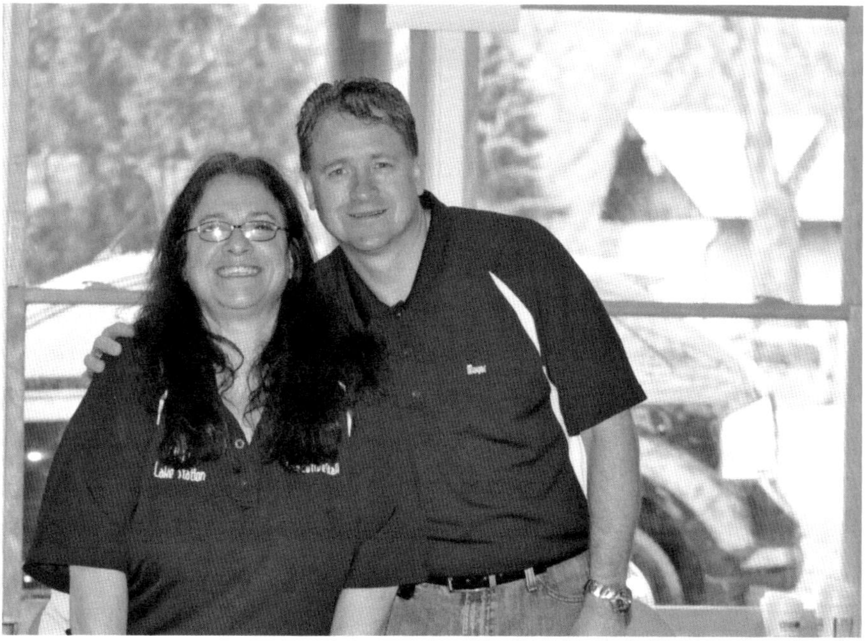

Former Lake Station mayor Keith Soderquist with his wife, Deborah Soderquist. *Courtesy of Lake Station City Hall.*

the Soderquists stole the cash "for personal expenses, including gambling activities at casinos in Indiana and Michigan."

"The feds don't indict someone unless they know they'll win the case," Anderson said, echoing many other Lake County public officials.

In July 2016, Capp announced that Brakley, thirty-six, was sentenced in Hammond Federal Court for one count of theft of government funds. She was sentenced to only two years of probation, which included a six-month term of home detention. She also was ordered to make restitution to the city of Lake Station in the amount of $664. There was public outrage when this news was released.

"I couldn't believe it," Frizzell said.

On September 28, U.S. District Court judges Rudy Lozano and James Moody sentenced Soderquist to forty-eight months in prison and his wife to twenty-four months, in addition to paying $4,184 in restitution to the city and $22,571 to the IRS, according to court documents. Six months of Soderquist's sentence was for trying to cover up his stepdaughter's crimes.

At the sentencing hearing, Judge Moody publicly scolded Soderquist by calling his crime against a food pantry "obscene." Moody said, "I've sentenced many politicians in my forty years, but what you have done is…shame on you. What the hell were you thinking? Are you goofy? Answer me."

Soderquist had nothing to say. He began serving his four-year sentence in mid-October 2016.

In the wake of the Soderquist family's crimes, Anderson, Frizzell and other city employees are left to pick up the pieces and try to rebuild the city's image

Lake Station Chamber of Commerce vice-president David Schmelzer had no easy answers when I met with him and Anderson in mid-2016.

"It's been a public relations nightmare," Schmelzer admitted.

"Every time we seem to remove ourselves from it, something pops back up in the newspapers," said Anderson, who is doing his best to learn the mayoral ropes after being elected to the office.

One of his first campaign promises had already taken root. He insisted on total transparency with city government actions. This includes joining the area's Shared Ethics Advisory Commission, which may appear more symbolic than anything, but it's an important, tangible step for this long-dysfunctional city.

"In the short months since Chris has taken over, we've seen 1,000 percent more cooperation and interest in chamber related functions. He's taken a

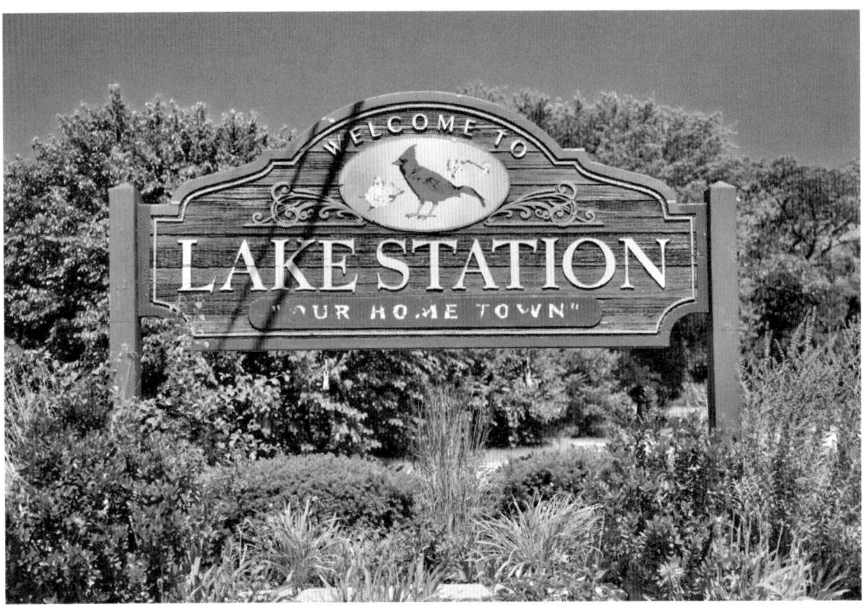

Lake Station welcome sign. *Courtesy of Joey Lax-Salinas.*

position as honorary board of director and he has attended our meetings to get involved with our activities," said Schmelzer, who like Anderson was born and raised in the city.

Over the past few years, Lake Station has been as divided and contentious as any other city in northwest Indiana. Some residents can't even agree on the city's very name, which has early origins as a train stop station in Lake County—Lake Station—until it was renamed East Gary in 1908, to lure U.S. Steel mill executives. In 1977, the city was renamed again Lake Station, which now boasts roughly fourteen thousand residents.

"We know our city has black eyes. We're trying to get off the mat," Schmelzer said.

8
Porter County
Political Seepage into Coffee Creek

In 1999, political sewage from Lake County seeped into Porter County through a little-known creek-centered development south of Chesterton. Near that small town, on the east side of State Road 49, a sprawling nature-centered development is hard to miss, with its water fountain, walking trails and pavilion amenities. Visitors from across the region visit here for parties, weddings, nature walks and picturesque photo shoots. Well-designed structures house a few businesses, flanked by several "McMansions" that have sprouted up through the years.

Beyond its scenic beauty, however, is a shady scandal involving fraud, conspiracy, bribes, kickbacks and an all-too-familiar name from Lake County machine politics. The crumbled roadway bricks that lead to the Coffee Creek Center offer a reminder of the development's nadir amid a foundation of hope and promise from almost twenty years earlier.

In the 1990s, a group of developers, investors and realtors had a broad vision encompassing 640 acres on that site. Early plans called for a 15,000-square-foot medical center, a multi-building apartment complex, 3 to 5 million square feet of commercial space and up to two thousand residential units within the pedestrian-friendly center. The idea was to attract working-class families and upscale professionals who could walk or ride bicycles to the center's retail stores conveniently located just around the corner. But even this pie-in-the-sky "new urbanism" attracted political-minded vultures who wanted a piece of the pie. Who better to slice it up than Lake County powerbrokers and politicians?

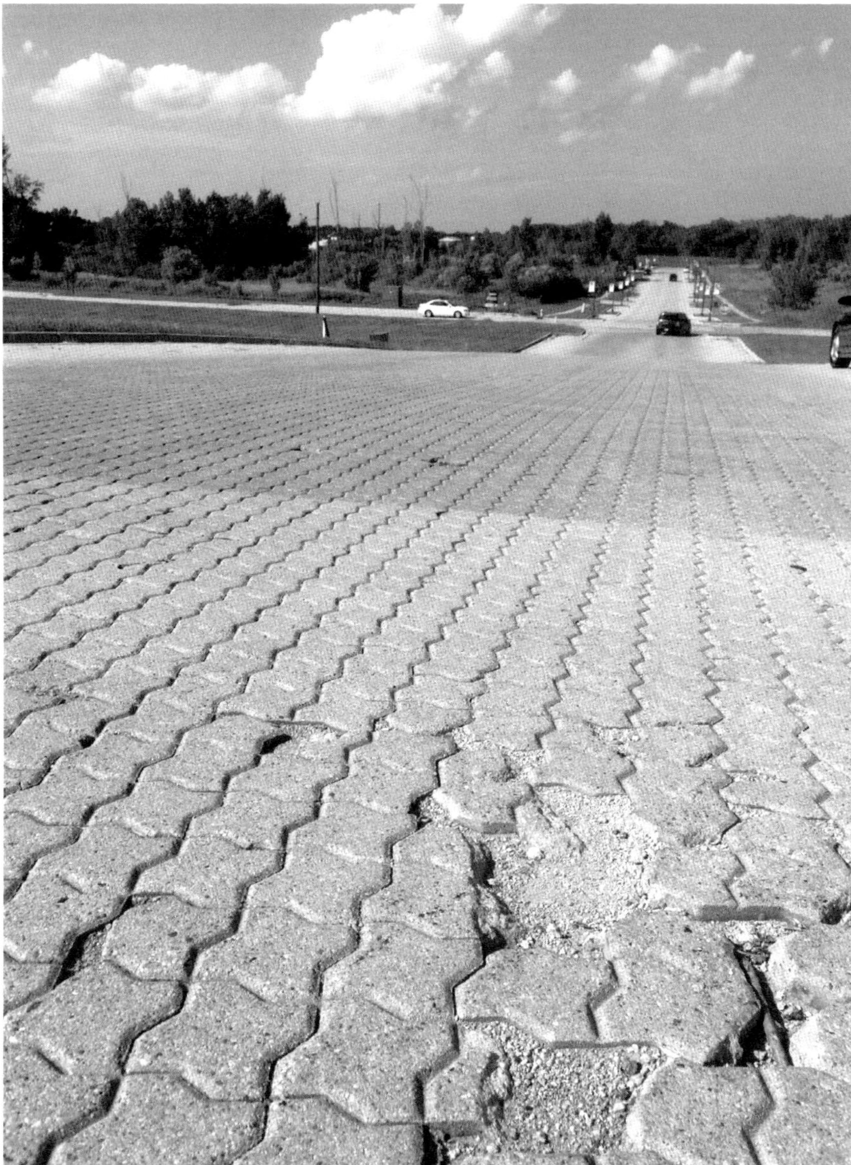

Coffee Creek development, Chesterton, Indiana. *Author's collection.*

This included former Indiana Democratic Party chairman Peter Manous, a Merrillville attorney who began his career as a grunt in the muscular Lake County arm of the organization. Manous and his family have ties

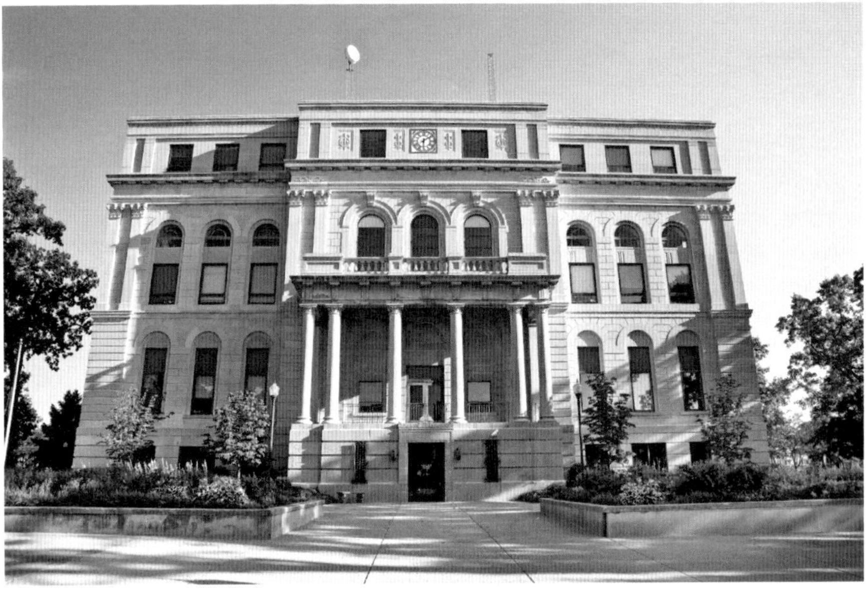

Porter County Courthouse, Valparaiso, Indiana. *Courtesy of Joey Lax-Salinas.*

going back to the Indiana Harbor section of East Chicago, including ties to the city's notorious Pastrick family. Manous's friendship with Kevin Pastrick, son of former East Chicago mayor Robert Pastrick, would prove to be an ominous one with this mixed-use development. At that time, Kevin Pastrick was a land developer and real estate broker who worked for Lake Erie Land Company, a subsidiary of NiSource. The scandal also involved Gerry Nannenga, former head of the Indiana Regional Council of Carpenters, who voted with the majority of its board to buy fifty-five acres within the development.

Manous and Nannenga both steered the Carpenters Pension Board toward the investment property, provided by the handiwork of Kevin Pastrick. It cost $10 million, of which Pastrick received a $600,000 sale commission, according to a thirty-five-page federal indictment. Of that sales commission, Pastrick gave kickbacks to both Manous and Nannenga, federal agents say.

In the simplest of terms, the purpose of the crime was to persuade the union to buy the land at an unreasonably high price and then secretly—and illegally—kick back a portion of the sales money to the three conspirators. The three men also set up a phony company and bank account to launder their ill-gotten windfall, prosecutors say.

At one time, Manous led a promising political career, even helping former Indiana governor Frank O'Bannon win elections in 1996 and 2000. In between those election wins, Manous's fingerprints could be found all over the union investment scandal. In 2002, federal prosecutors began exploring details behind the questionable land deal. Several indictments were issued, alleging that the three men met in the summer of 1998.

Manous would later admit in court that he betrayed the trust of many people, and the union, pleading guilty to eight felony counts. He also admitted to creating fake business documents, lying to investigators with the U.S. Department of Labor and trying to cover up the scandal with more lies. Before he went to trial, Manous faced forty-four years in prison and $1.75 million in fines. After selling out his friend Pastrick, Manous testified against him, serving only twenty-seven months in prison and paying $125,000 in restitution.

Nannenga stepped down as head of the Indiana Regional Council of Carpenters before serving eighteen months in prison. As for Pastrick, believed to be the mastermind behind the deal, he served three years in prison and was fined $177,500. While awaiting sentencing, police say Pastrick was arrested in a prostitution sting in South Bend, Indiana. Those charges were later dropped. In 2006, while incarcerated, he claimed he was bankrupt

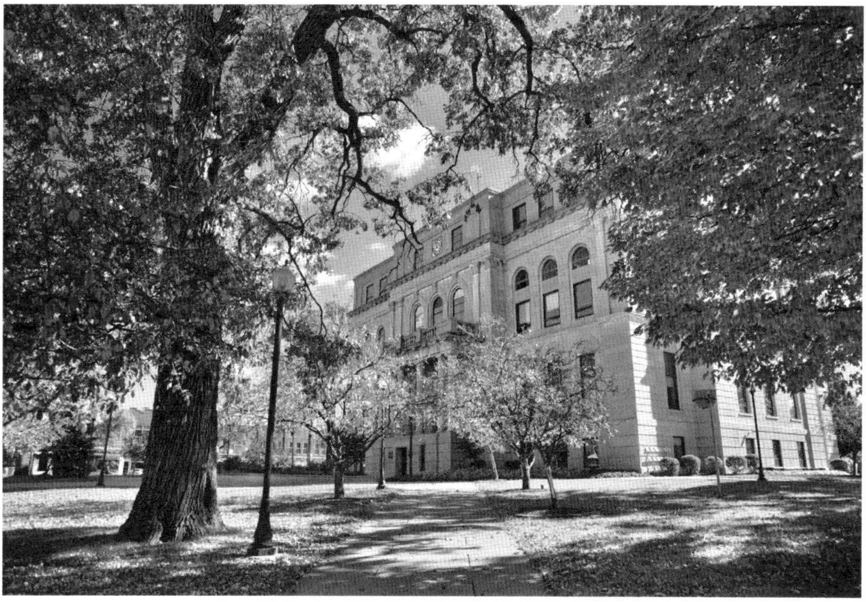

Porter County Courthouse, Valparaiso, Indiana. *Courtesy of Joey Lax-Salinas.*

and didn't have money to pay his attorney, let alone his legal settlement. According to his LinkedIn social media page in 2016, he has since returned to work in "corporate sales."

This eye-opening case in comparatively sleepy Porter County prompted front-page headlines for months. Still, it was one of the few cases that reflected Lake County's notorious reputation of public corruption. As one longtime prosecuting attorney in Porter County told me, "I can't think of any acts of corruption that are in the same universe as what has transpired in Lake County."

Dan Whitten, a Porter County–based attorney and Porter County councilman, has served in several public positions with the military, law enforcement and elected office.

"In each of these chapters of my life, I have happened upon people who have breached the trust given them," Whitten said. "I am always astounded and disappointed because I believe public service is a relationship built in trust. When a public servant changes course and becomes more of a personal servant, thus serving his or her own interests over those of the public, it is not just a betrayal of the people he or she serves but also a betrayal of those they serve with. The damage cannot be quantified."

Whitten added:

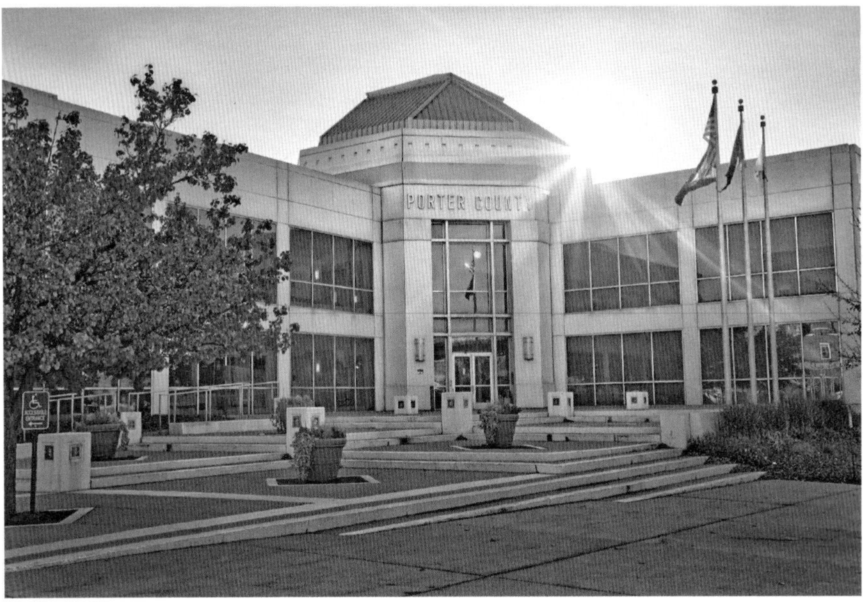

Porter County Government Center, Valparaiso, Indiana. *Courtesy of Joey Lax-Salinas.*

The thing that I find somewhat consistent is that unlike many other areas of life, corrupt public officials seem to have, in many cases, taken a risk that far outweighs their potential gain. Even when I scratch my head and try to understand the thinking of someone who is clearly operating with their moral compass pointed south, I just don't understand what possible cost-benefit analysis could have been in their heads. They have endeavored upon a path that, if all went well, would bring very little gain, with potential great loss. They are in fact placing their public and private lives at risk against the potential for a very small, very shortsighted gain. It must lead me to the conclusion that a dishonest elected official or public servant is nothing more than a dishonest person who has found their way to a public-service arena.

Part III

Efforts Through the Decades to Curb Political Crime

9

Shared Ethics Advisory Commission

If you have to ask if what you are doing is wrong...it probably is.
—Indiana Supreme Court justice Robert Rucker

Governmental ethics in Lake County?

I couldn't help but ponder this long-running oxymoron while attending a heavily-attended Northwest Indiana Ethics Summit. Hosted by the Shared Ethics Advisory Commission, it attracted nearly three hundred guests, featuring a who's who of movers, shakers and policymakers in this region. Together, they dissected the word *ethics* and how it applies to specific

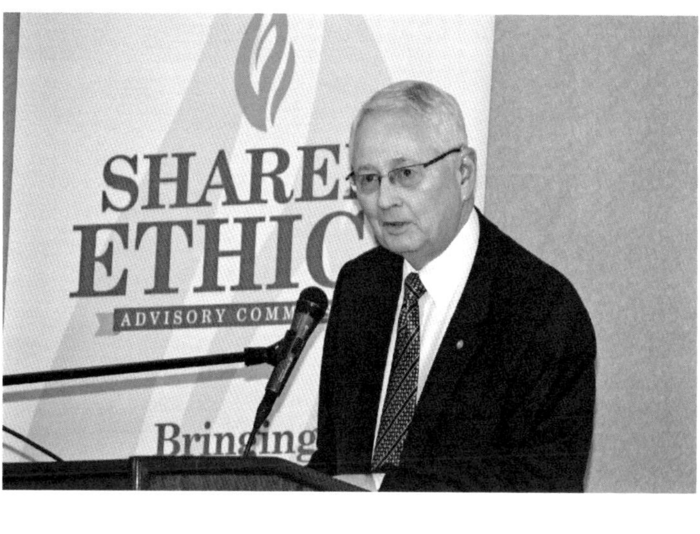

Calvin Bellamy, president of Shared Ethics Advisory Commission. *Courtesy of Shared Ethics Advisory Commission.*

case studies and real-life situations, with input from a panel of experts: Chesterton town manager Bernie Doyle, Lake County attorney Marce Gonzalez and Ellen Szarleta, director of the Indiana University Northwest Center for Urban and Regional Excellence.

"Our goal is to raise awareness," explained Calvin Bellamy, president of the Shared Ethics Advisory Commission. "Ethics training needs to be reinforced, like safety training."

The three-county commission, designed to train northwest Indiana officials on ethical decision making, marked its ten-year anniversary at that event. At the time, it had eighteen communities signed up. Before the summit, Bellamy told me more than four hundred candidates in the primary election races had signed the 2015 Candidate Ethics Action Pledge.

"Lake County having more, by far, than the other two counties combined," he said.

This was welcome news for Lake County voters. Every Election Day is their best opportunity to vote for, or against, public officeholders whose ethics are questionable or nonexistent. Ethics has many definitions, and my favorite version has always been this one: doing the right thing when no one is watching. I couldn't help but wonder how many of our political leaders live up to that definition on a daily basis, including many who attended that ethics summit.

During Bellamy's opening remarks, two large screens flanking his podium showed a cartoon regarding ethics. It got a few laughs, but it's no laughing matter that our corner of the state is the butt of endless jokes about our cartoonish reputation regarding ethics in government. Bellamy deflected this obvious fact by noting that the Shared Ethics Advisory Commission was garnering renewed attention from across the state for its efforts to change our shady reputation.

"We're a busy group, and we're here to set the tone for an ethics culture," he told the audience.

This effort can be a challenge, or an illusion, in a county that's been littered with corrupt public officials through the decades. Most recently, before this event, Lake County surveyor George Van Til was sentenced to eighteen months in prison for public corruption. Calumet Township trustee Mary Elgin, along with three aides, was indicted the previous year on public corruption charges. And Lake Station mayor Keith Soderquist was waiting to stand trial for charges involving misuse of public funds.

What's behind such chronic betrayal of governmental ethics? Is it delusions of power? A drunken arrogance of public office? A warped sense of entitlement? "I confess no expertise on ethics," admitted Indiana Supreme Court justice Robert D. Rucker, who served as the event's keynote speaker.

Rucker is a Gary native who received his law degree from Valparaiso University in 1976, served as a Lake County deputy prosecutor and, in 1999, was appointed as an Indiana Supreme Court justice. "I'm honored to be home again," he told guests before attempting to define the complexities of ethics in public office and legal cases.

The dictionary defines it as a system of moral principles or the rules of conduct recognized in respect to a particular group. More broadly, it is a branch of philosophy dealing in respect to the rightness and wrongness of certain actions.

Rucker, whose speech was laced with self-effacing humor, acknowledged that even he can be intimidated by the mere "notion of ethics."

"There's no air-tight definition," he said. "But we know it when we see it."

He used real-life examples to illustrate his point that it's not always as simple as right versus wrong. But "right versus right" regards such shades of gray as justice versus mercy, truth versus duty and short-term good versus long-term good. "Which side trumps the other?" he asked rhetorically.

For most northwest Indiana residents, ethics in public office simply means doing your job without corrupting the office you've been elected to hold. Is that asking too much? In this region, yes, apparently it is. Before the summit began, I talked with a few guests about the notion of ethics, as Rucker called it. They didn't ponder its abstract nature, complex dilemmas or academic discourse, as Rucker touched on. Instead, they immediately and instinctively zeroed in on its lack of existence in too many public offices across Lake County.

This lack is not solely the realm of the aforementioned elected officials who have been charged, convicted or sentenced but the laundry list of others who have served before them. And by served I mean first serving the public and then serving time behind bars for their crimes while in office. It's so commonplace here that we make bets which public official will be indicted next.

It all comes down to decisions and consequences. What should I do? What is right? What is wrong? Ethics in the abstract is a noble ideal, and everyone clamors in agreement. Ethics in public office, however, is a different story. It's when rubber meets the road, intersecting at the busy crossroads of idealism and realism. More specifically, it concerns what should I do versus what will I do. It comes back to fostering what Bellamy called a culture of ethics in northwest Indiana. Citizens—especially long-frustrated ones—can play a crucial, even pivotal, role in this process, which is exactly what took place in the Calumet region, particularly in Gary, during the late 1940s and 1950s.

10
Women's Citizens Committee

On March 7, 1949, roughly 2,000 women gathered at Seaman Hall in Gary to form the Women's Citizens Committee, or the WCC," according to a historical article in the Calumet Regional Archives at Indiana University Northwest. "Having felt that Mary Cheever's death was the last straw in their tolerance of crime and corruption in Gary, the women left Seaman Hall and marched towards City Hall, where a council meeting was taking place."

The women crowded into Gary City Hall chambers to demand law and order in the Steel City. After three hours of heated exchanges, the angry women still weren't satisfied. During a ten-minute recess in the meeting, a chorus of women shouted, "Block the doorways! Don't let 'em out of here," according to a story in the *Northwest Indiana Sentinel*.

Cheever was a Lew Wallace language teacher who was murdered that year.

"My high school history teacher, Hazel Grieger, who was a friend of Mary Cheever, was active in the Women's Citizens Committee and the Gary Crime Commission in the aftermath of that murder," said Kendall Svengalis, a Gary native who authored the 2006 book *Gary, Indiana: A Centennial Celebration*.

"The incident exposed, for many, the deeper layers of crime in Gary, including prostitution and vice generally," Svengalis added.

According to the Calumet Archives article, written by Jennifer M. Grecco, "The women demanded that Gary was to be cleaned up. The mayor, Eugene H. Swartz, was given a time limit of two weeks to rid Gary of its

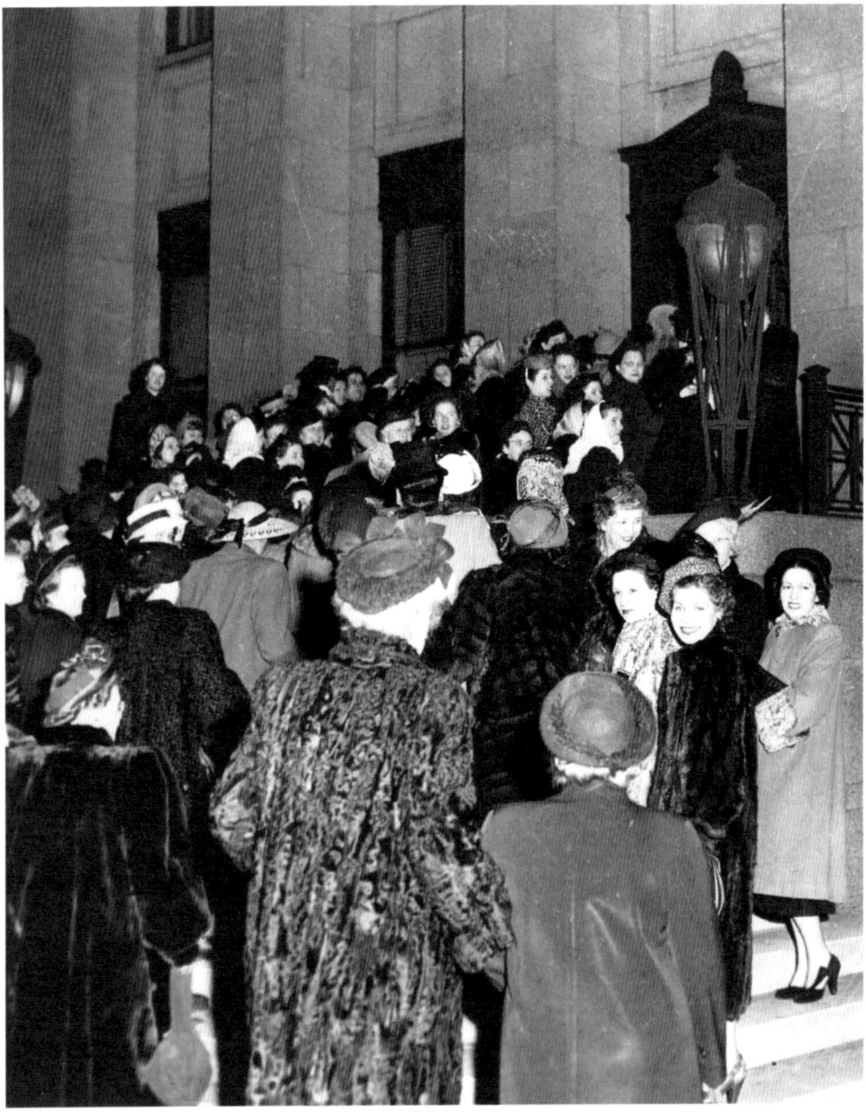

Women's Citizen Committee's march on Gary City Hall, March 7, 1949. *Courtesy of Calumet Regional Archives.*

vice. As spokesman for the WCC, Ida K. Saks declared, 'It's up to you to do something and do it quickly.' If the council didn't act, the WCC would call upon the governor."

By March 14, 1949, the WCC had established an executive committee, consisting of twenty-one members, plus a board of delegates representing three hundred women's groups. On March 25 of that year, a delegation of women visited Indiana governor Henry F. Schricker to discuss Gary's rampant problems. In July 1949, the WCC launched a program called "Operation Shoe Leather," leading hundreds of volunteers to picket brothels, salons and gambling houses. By 1950, the WCC was more concerned with political action to achieve their goals, leading an effort to oust Benjamin Schwartz, the incumbent Lake County prosecutor.

"The WCC also sponsored a crime commission modeled after a private Chicago organization," the archives article states. "The Crime Commission bugged the office of Deputy Prosecutor Blaz A. Lucas. Publishing '*The Microphone Speaks*,' the WCC and Crime Commission made public the conversations between Lucas and Jack Doyle, and Lucas and other racketeers. The WCC campaigned for David Stanton effortlessly. He was victorious, but soon encountered problems with Lake Criminal Court Judge William J. Murray."

"In 1951, the WCC was concerned with city elections," the article continues.

> *WCC officer Hylda Burton ran in the primaries for the Democratic ticket as mayor. She came in third. Peter Mandich (a Democrat) won, and surprised reformers by naming James Traeger as police chief. However, Traeger was fired. The WCC was adamantly opposed to the administration since Mandich claimed they were no threat.*
>
> *By 1952, Metro Holovachka was victorious over Stanton. Holovachka was not interested in dealing with the WCC. Because of negative feedback, the WCC energies began to slow down. However, "On January 19, 1954, the WCC forced the city council to hold hearings after a nine-year-old child was molested near Froebel School."*

By then, the national spotlight shone on Gary and its tarnished reputation beyond its Steel City image. Several magazines featured cover stories on all the crime and the crime-fighting women's group. Headlines screamed: "The Great Gary Cleanup," in *McCalls*, 1951; "The Angry Housewives of Gary," in *Cornet* magazine, 1951; "What Women Did in Gary," in *Ladies' Home Journal* from that same year; "Steeltown Sin," in *Man to Man* magazine, 1955; "How We Cleaned Up Gary," in *Male* magazine, 1953; and "Steel and Sex," in *Quick* magazine, 1955.

Still, in the July 23, 1955 issue of the *Chicago Daily News*, a headline stated, "Dice, Cards, Girls—Reform Getting Nowhere in Gary."

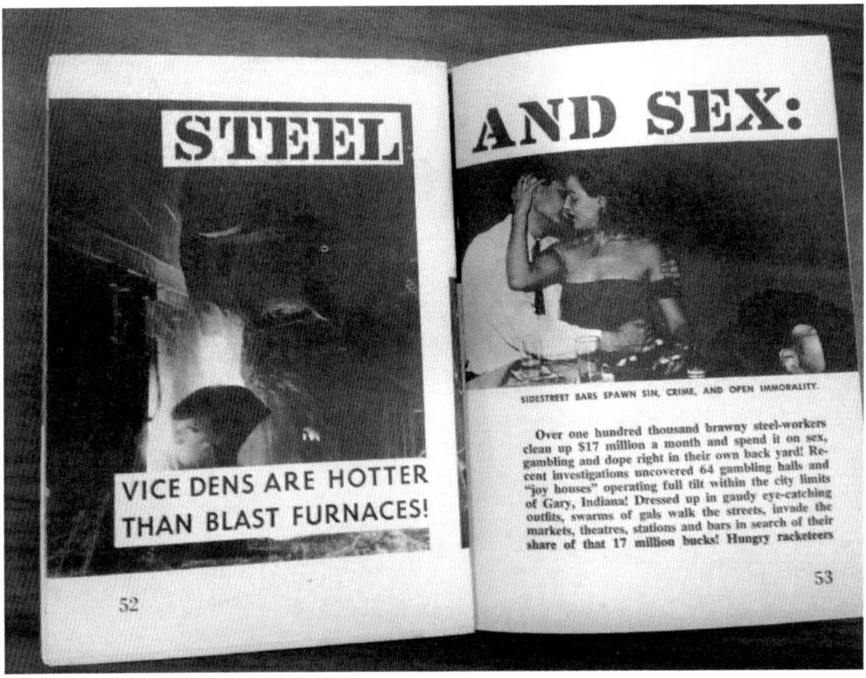

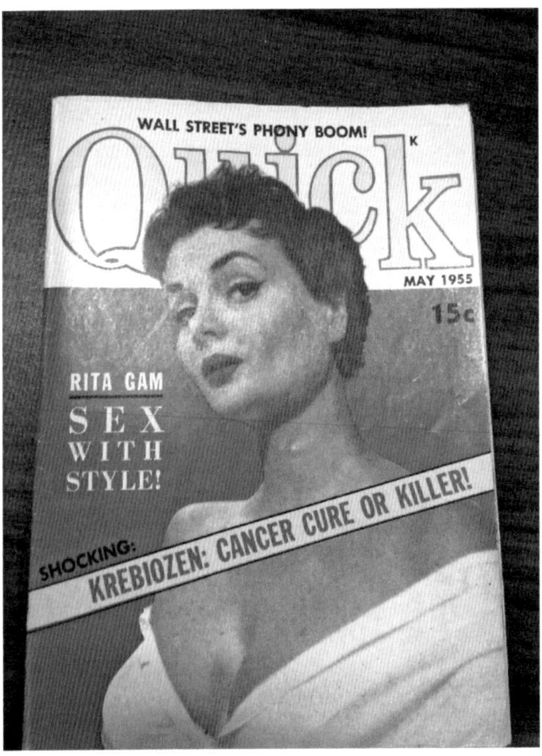

Above: *Quick* magazine story: "Steel and Sex in Gary, Indiana," May 1955. *Courtesy of Calumet Regional Archives.*

Left: *Quick* magazine cover, May 1955. *Courtesy of Calumet Regional Archives.*

"Despite strong setbacks, the WCC continued to strive....Said Mrs. Alma Mackall, chairman of the WCC, in the 'Dice, Cards Girls...' article in the *Chicago Daily News*, "Well, it may be discouraging but we're not going to give up."

11
Northwest Indiana Crime Commission

By 1959, the WCC had gotten involved in investigating countywide corruption in Lake County with the Northwest Indiana Crime Commission. The group was formed in June 1959 with the stated purpose "to expose graft and rackets and reestablish good government through good law enforcement," according to its August 1962 thirty-two-page report.

"The syndicate has a good thing here," said Francis E. Lynch, who was named operating director of the NWI Crime Commission in January 1961. "It won't be chased out easily."

The Crime Commission's "statement of purpose" outlined its intentions: "It is not the business of the Crime Commission to take over the functions of the police, the prosecutor and other officials. Our job is to act as an agent of all the people of this community by seeing to it all officials perform their duty. No right thinking official will object to receiving assistance. Any official who resents observation of his work must have something to hide."

Page one of the report states, "The Northwest Indiana Crime Commission presents this booklet as a public service to the people of Lake and Porter counties, Indiana. It is the hope of the Commission that this resume of conditions as we have found them, and report of what has been accomplished to date, will merit your continued interest and support."

"Scandal is no stranger to Lake County," the report continues on page five.

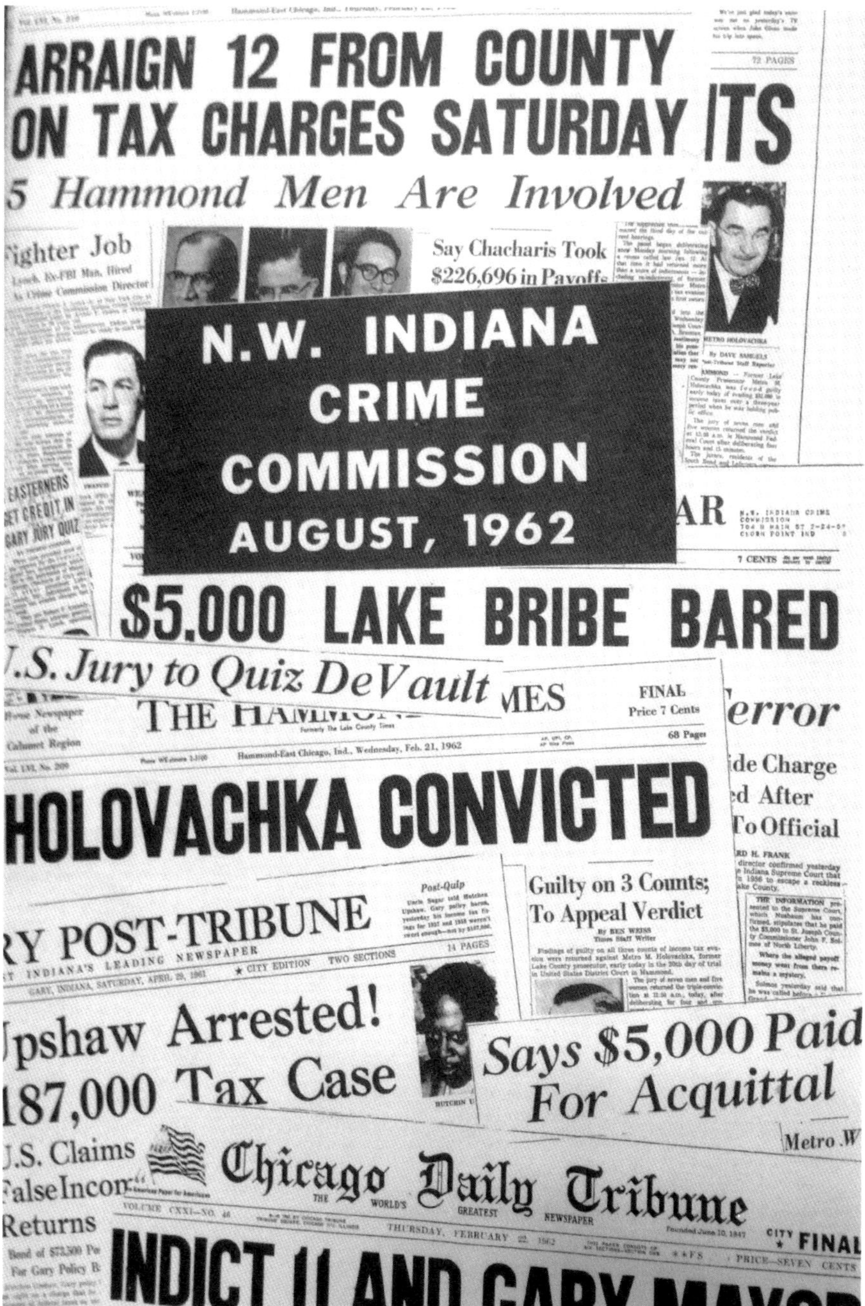

Northwest Indiana Crime Commission report, 1962. *Author's collection.*

> *Perhaps the prevalence of crime in a community develops a tolerance for it. When gambling, robberies, killings, prostitution and all other kinds of crime were confined within certain areas of the community, good citizens may have been apathetic. But when a United States Senate investigation focused nationwide attention on the crime and 'public corruption' in Northwest Indiana, citizens aroused at last, met in a great indignation rally to form the Northwest Indiana Crime Commission...a non-political, non-partisan organization to serve as a permanent force opposing crime and corruption.*

In September 1961, Herald S. Swaim, a retiring Gary police captain, was named chief investigator of the new organization.

"Much of the success of the initial steps in the organization of the Crime Commission is due to the efforts of Arthur F. Endres who assumed the leadership of the group and led the way to the establishment of a well-functioning commission," the highly detailed report notes.

On June 2, 1959, Senator John McClellan, chairman of the U.S. Senate Committee, said, "The committee today begins an inquiry of certain activities in Lake County, Indiana. During the more than two years of the committee's existence, it has found itself squarely faced with the problem of public corruption. Such has again proved to be the case in Lake County, Indiana."

In 1961, when Lynch began his investigation, he interviewed Lake County prosecutor Floyd Vance, Gary police chief John Foley, Hammond police chief Michael Kambiss and other law enforcement officials. Lynch hoped by doing so he could get to the bottom of the county's corruption problems and, just as importantly, determine why no one was being held accountable for questionable behavior or flat-out criminal actions.

No one, however, was willing to talk to Lynch. And if he was able to interview someone, Lynch, an outsider, was met with blanket denials that any wrongdoing or corruption was taking place. "It became clear to me," Lynch noted in his six-month report, "that local police and the prosecutor had neither the desire nor the 'know-how' to get the job done."

> *From what I have learned since my arrival here, it is my considered opinion there is a general breakdown in government throughout Lake County. Morale is low and performance is very poor among the police departments and the sheriff's department. Bribery and shakedowns are endemic on all levels of government. In Gary, there appears to be a distinct possibility of a total collapse in the work department. Other police departments and the sheriff's*

office are seriously hampered by the political interference and operate under the direction of political persons neither equipped with knowledge of law enforcement, nor motivated by the desire of impartial administration of justice. This carries over into the work of the prosecuting attorney's office and the county criminal court.

In September 1961, Robert F. Kennedy, attorney general of the United States who had served as chief counsel of the McClellan Committee, appointed a special assistant U.S. attorney to investigate, indict and prosecute violations of federal law in Lake County. This appointment was given to Jay Goldberg.

"Mr. Goldberg came to Lake County and immediately began to work with officials of the Justice Department, particularly Special Agents of the Internal Revenue Service and the FBI," the report explains.

Goldberg's investigation led to several indictments ordered from a federal grand jury on February 21, 1962, including Gary mayor George Chacharis, Lake County sheriff Peter Mandich and Gary city engineer Harold Zweig, among several other public officials in Gary and Hammond.

"These indictments are not frivolous, empty charges," Lynch publicly announced at the time. "These indictments tend to prove what the Crime Commission knows as fact, corruption is endemic in Lake County. The indictments… indicate corruption in the public life of Lake County. This is shocking to all honest citizens regardless of party affiliation. Corruption is like an iceberg; most of it remains hidden."

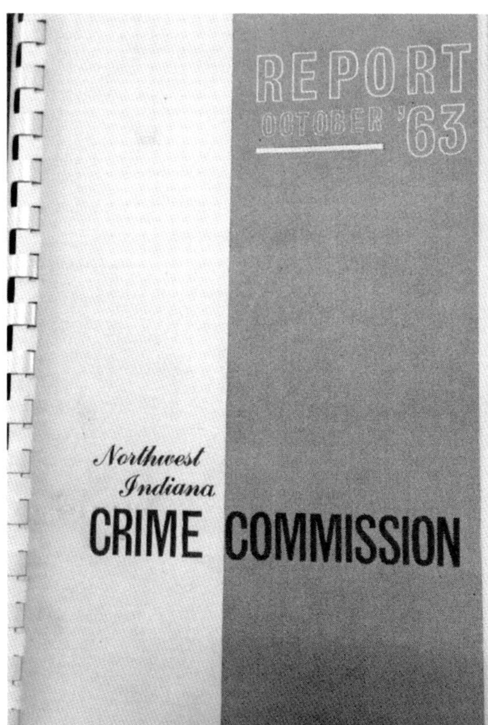

Northwest Indiana Crime Commission report, 1963. *Author's collection.*

McClellan wrote, "The illicit operations which appear

to have flourished in Lake County since 1950 would have been impossible without the knowledge, acquiescence, and cooperation of some public officials....It is historic that where law enforcement falls down, it is an open invitation to hoodlums and racketeers to move in and operate. That this occurred in Lake County, Indiana, is clear from the evidence."

At the annual Crime Commission dinner in June 1962, Lynch told guests, "When the local officials enter into an alliance with the corrupt elements of the community, there is really no one for the citizen to turn to. He simply becomes the victim of such corruption."

"It's now up to the local officials, and here you and I and the Crime Commission have a great deal of work to do. We shall continue to give the benefit of our attention to the prosecutor's office, the various police departments, and carefully selected individuals who continue to hold high office," he said.

"This Crime Commission and this work we are attempting to do obviously is not for everyone," Lynch wrote in the report. "We are in deep water, we are engaged in a tough fight and the game sometimes gets dirty. It is not for everyone. It had always been astounding to me that so few good people really care."

Meanwhile, the WCC was slowing down its efforts for reform after years of public confrontation and personal frustration. "The women were just plain tired," states the article in the Calumet Regional Archives. "As Beryl Brownell said in a June 21, 1989, interview, the group was exhausted and feeling very defeated. When the Crime Commission joined forces with the WCC, according to Miss Brownell, it was the beginning of the end for the WCC. The men of the Crime Commission began a secret chase to beat organized crime at their own game. A plan, according to Miss Brownell, that helped to hurt the reformers' effort in the end."

Other efforts through the years attempted to thwart this region's chronic corruption issues while bolstering ethics in local government. Some public awareness campaigns were better organized and longer lasting than others.

"Public corruption is a plague that infects all that it touches," wrote current state senator Ed Charbonneau in May 2005, to introduce a sixteen-page document titled "A Changing Culture: Ethical Government in Northwest Indiana."

> *It not only corrupts those involved, but corrupts the system of government that permits it to survive. It corrupts the area where it exists and taints the view that those outside the area have. It corrupts the public's confidence in*

their elected officials and causes the public to not participate in the political process with the view that it makes no difference because everyone is corrupt.

Does it sound familiar to the earlier campaigns from the Crime Commission and WCC? The report continues:

For far too long, citizens looked at corrupt government as a way of doing business in Lake County. Tolerance of corrupt public officials resulted in even lower expectations. This image unfortunately tends to become self-fulfilling and makes any effort to change it all the more difficult. Long characterized as a place where government corruption was the norm rather than the exception, a culture change of epic proportions is taking place in Northwest Indiana....

Although the vast majority of public officials in the region are honest and ethical, over the years, everyone gets tainted, and ultimately all pay a heavy price for those who are in public service for personal gain. As the new millennium arrived, that all began to change in Northwest Indiana as a major "weeding and seeding" effort began to unfold. Public disgust had reached a point where business as usual was no longer acceptable.

Beginning in 1990, a series of events eventually led to the incorporation in 2000 of the Northwest Indiana Quality of Life Council, which served as the impetus for change.

"To date, many cities, towns, and other governmental units in Northwest Indiana have recognized the importance of ethical government to the quality of life, capital investment, and job creation in the region," the Changing Culture report states. It continues:

They have taken that belief and acted on it by adopting ethics ordinances or ethics policies. Many others have come to realize it is in their best interests to get involved and become part of the solution, while others steadfastly refuse to adopt the concept of ethics in government. The weeding has started and will continue, but if simply prosecuting and locking up those public officials who abuse the public trust was the answer, Lake County and Northwest Indiana would long ago have become a corruption-free zone. This obviously is not the sole answer. Significant culture changing activity—the seeding—has occurred over the past two to three years. In the author's opinion, there is more being done in Northwest Indiana on a regional basis to promote a climate of renewed confidence in public

> *officials than anywhere else in the country. Just a few short years ago, none of this would even have been considered. The citizens are standing up and becoming the good gardeners.*

Calvin Bellamy, president of the Shared Ethics Advisory Commission, has been working hard to recruit more "good gardeners" by challenging the existing culture and encouraging public officials to stop and think about the consequences of their actions.

"I would argue that corrupt officials are being weeded out more rapidly, by voters when they can tell what's going on and, in other cases, by the U.S. general attorney. If a mayor misbehaves, for example, people are in a better position to know how to respond. We are trying to build a new culture, but changing engrained habits is a very long process," Bellamy said.

The Shared Ethics Advisory Commission was created in 2005 with three member communities: Munster, Highland and Crown Point. As recently as 2012, it had only seven municipal members. By mid-2016, it boasted twenty-three out of a possible forty-four communities in the three-county (Lake, Porter and LaPorte) region.

"We think we may be the only agency, perhaps in the country, that is working on ethics training on a regional basis, organized as a group of the

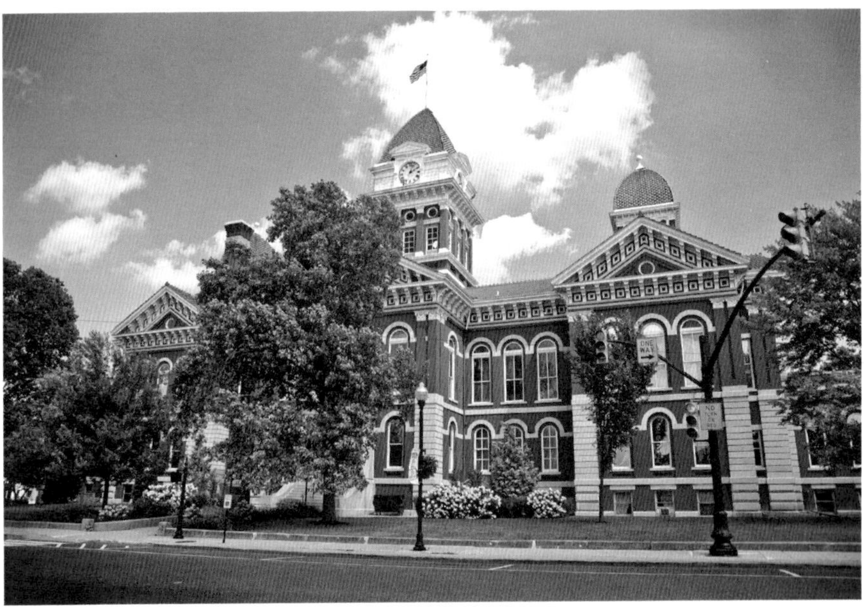

Former Lake County Courthouse, Crown Point, Indiana. *Courtesy of Joey Lax-Salinas.*

willing," Bellamy said. "We have no way to require membership. Usually, I find some way to get before a city council or mayor and, sometimes, it takes many visits and even several years to close the deal."

"I think Cal Bellamy has the right approach," said Lake County historian Bruce Woods. "Ask political bodies to join, educate them through seminars, and hope it will put pressure on those who do not join in."

The group's inter-local agreement that creates the commission specifically excludes elected officials and also prohibits it from issuing advisory opinions or adjudicating disputes. "Our assigned mission is to train public employees on ethical decision making," Bellamy said. "Fortunately, elected officials often attend our training sessions."

At the group's first Ethics Summit, Andy Shaw from the Better Government Association of Chicago was its keynote speaker. "His group is a watchdog group. We are a training group," Bellamy said. A training group establishes expectations. A watchdog group sees if those expectations are being met. "Twice, I have tried to help a local watchdog group get started, but nothing came of it," Bellamy said.

The commission focuses on public employees more than it does on elected officials.

"We're not designed to weed out criminal behavior," Bellamy noted. "We focus on ethics, which sometimes involves criminal acts and sometimes is really about best practices. Despite our limitations, I think we have had some success in raising the visibility of ethics and that may be having a positive effect in general."

"We do not deal in criminal matters. We are simply in the business of trying to help public employees understand the challenges they face, help them stop and think, and maybe help each other reach a higher standard," Bellamy said. "We know we are just a piece in the puzzle, but it is hard to hold people to a standard if no one ever tells them what that standard is. That seems to be the indispensable first step in holding people to a higher standard."

Bellamy and his board understand that even specially trained officials and employees can still conduct unethical behavior. For those individuals, such training simply doesn't work, they admit.

"Others may just be careless and do something wrong. But carelessness only points to the need for more training," Bellamy said.

Not everyone agrees with more ethics training or publicly signing a pledge.

"Unethical behavior has been a way of life for so many in the region that they sometimes don't even realize it's unethical. Signing an ethics

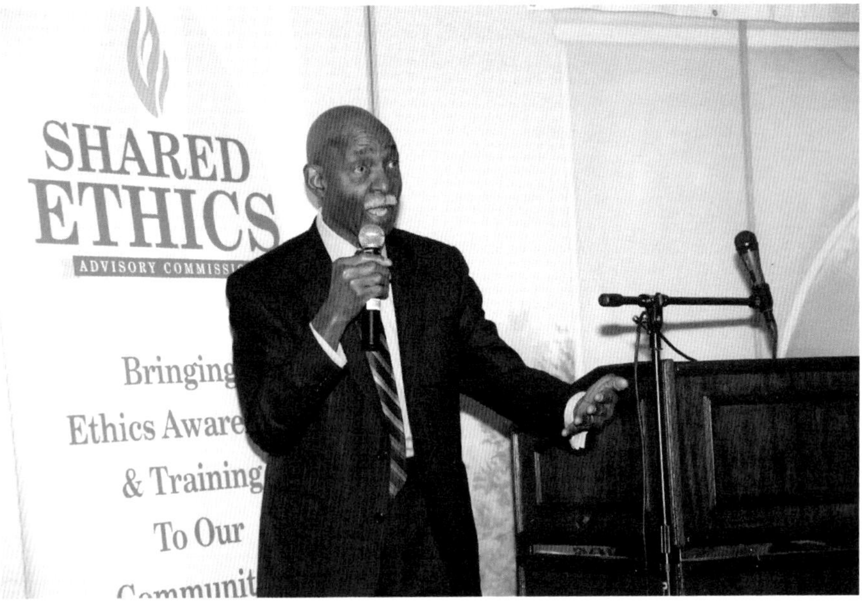

Indiana Supreme Court justice Robert Rucker speaks to the audience at the 2015 Ethics Summit on March 12, 2015, at Avalon Manor in Merrillville, Indiana. *Courtesy of Shared Ethics Advisory Commission.*

pledge doesn't change that," said Kim Krull, a longtime member of the Lake County Republican Party. "What would prompt change is having a non-partisan compliance officer in county government who local and county officials and workers can report to, and who has access to the U.S. Attorney's Office."

Indiana Supreme Court justice Robert D. Rucker readily admitted he was not an expert on the best definition of ethics. But he certainly had the best advice to public officials and elected officeholders in this region: "If you have to ask what you're doing is wrong…it probably is."

Part IV

Current Corruption and Future Remedies

12

Analysis from a Political Science Perspective

What's wrong with us in northwest Indiana?

We're strategically located at the often-hyped "crossroads of the country." We have natural resources that other regions envy. We bask in the shadow of America's third-largest city. And we have the potential—a foreign word for too many Hoosiers—to lead this historically backward state through

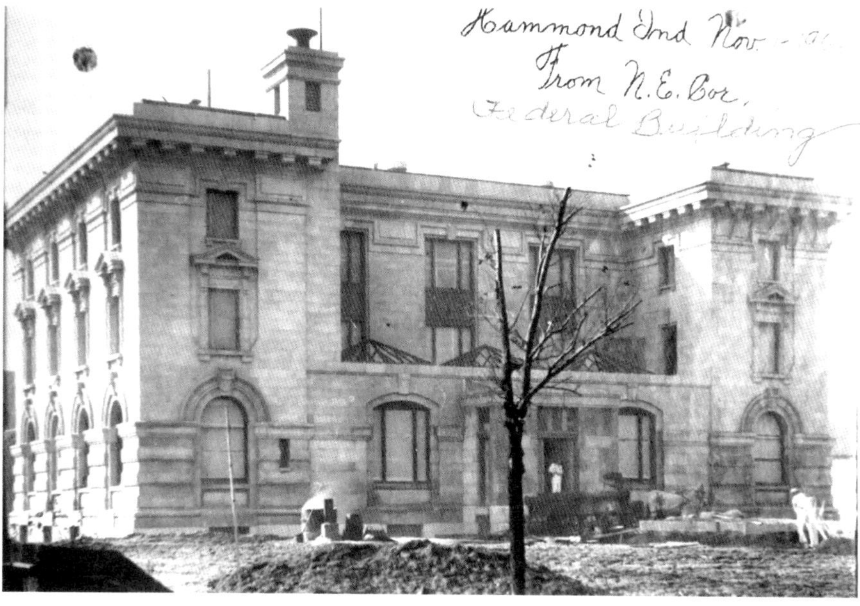

Old Federal Courthouse, Hammond, Indiana. *Courtesy of Hammond Public Library.*

the twenty-first century. Yet here we are, mired in twentieth-century politics, nineteenth-century prejudices and eighteenth-century belief systems.

As the late *Times* newspaper columnist Mark Kiesling once quipped, "Lake County voters punch a straight Democratic ticket because Franklin D. Roosevelt told them to."

We live with blinders on regarding progressive growth and global possibilities. We embrace our region's ugliness, pollution and stagnation while masking them with words such as *charming*, *productive* and *gritty*. We lack a singular vision that would unify our fragmented communities. And we not only tolerate political greed and corruption but also continually vote it back into office.

Prohibition was intended to be the "era of clear thinking and clean living," according to the Anti-Saloon League at the time. Instead, it turned out to be the catalyst that merged criminals and politicians together while making once-poor hoodlums rich and once-invisible politicos infamous.

"Location played a more definite role in the early days when people came over here from Illinois for horseracing or quickie marriages," said Lake County historian Bruce Woods.

The Chicago mob had its foot in Lake County, Indiana, since Prohibition days, paying off public officials with whiskey, kickbacks and women, not always in that order. Not all evil and vice was centered in Calumet City, where it had flourished so brazenly along the city's infamous "Strip." To this day, its dirty footprints can still be found in some political circles in Lake County government.

This has created a culture of greed, arrogance and entitlement, with too many elected officials and their political partners wanting a piece of the public projects pie.

"This is why big projects don't come here—the politics behind the projects," said one veteran political consultant.

Such thinking of entitlement trickled down to average workers, especially inside the many steel mills lining Lake Michigan shorelines. Previous generations of steelworkers used the mills as their personal hardware stores, thinking nothing of stealing tools, supplies and other equipment for personal use. It was nothing to order, say, six items for your department and sneak one of them away for yourself. This still goes on today in the steel mills and related factories, a systemic form of graft that reflects public corruption from our elected officials. Question is, how many elected or appointed officeholders are getting into public office to conduct criminal activity?

"Anyone who gets into public office with the intention of stealing from the taxpayers are extremely dumb people in my opinion," said Hammond mayor Thomas McDermott Jr. He continued:

> *Any elected official who has the mindset of personally enriching themselves, through the decisions they make on behalf of the taxpayers, deserves to be indicted. The fact that we all know the feds are actively looking closely at all decisions we make as elected officials makes it even harder to comprehend what goes through these people's minds when they get caught in improprieties. It's pure greed, a sense of entitlement and a cockiness that is hard to understand.*

McDermott once clerked for the U.S. Attorney's Office after his first year of law school. That summer, he attended more that fifty jury trials and watched federal attorneys conduct their daily work. He came away with an unforgettable lesson.

"I didn't see the feds lose once that entire summer," he said. "The feds never lose a case in court. Never."

Marie Eisenstein said that from a cultural perspective, not only is corruption expected, but there is also little belief that it can be mitigated in any way. "Part of what allows this cultural norm to continue, decade after decade, is a system that relies on traditional loyalty rather than on adherence to the rule of law. Remember, the United States is specifically founded on the notion of the rule of law; we are a nation of laws not of men."

Inherent or implied in her statement is that we have replaced the typical notions of loyalty that are "tribal" or "communal" with a commitment to the abstract rule of law. This can be defined by the argument that we will follow the rule of law regardless of who it is that is responsible for enforcing it, and the individual responsible for enforcing it will do so regardless of who the law must be enforced against, Eisenstein noted.

"Lake County has simply devolved, beginning in the 1930s and continuing unabated until present day, with a more tribal- or clan-like adherence to loyalty rather than a principled adherence to the rule of law," she said. "It is not only expected and accepted by the populace or citizenry, but deemed unchangeable."

"The post–World War II era, with its emphasis on federal social-welfare programs, decreased the role of a city machine doling out social welfare services in order to get votes," she said. "But that is not to say there are no divisible benefits that can be handed out. The machines that persisted post–World War II, and after the increase of federally funded

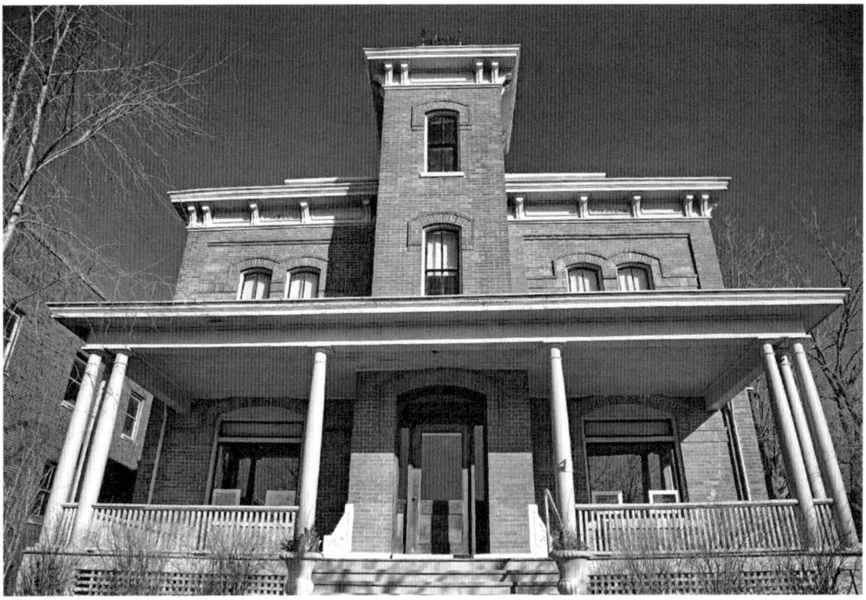

Former Lake County sheriff's house and jail, Crown Point, Indiana. *Courtesy of Joey Lax-Salinas.*

social welfare programs, did so in part by being in a position to administer and dispense those federal goodies and monies."

In social science, there are inevitably a multitude of variables that go into making government what it is, both structurally and socially. With that said, Eisenstein noted, there are some variables more important than others.

"There are, currently and historically, only two industries that provide any type of economic development in Lake County—steel and oil," Eisenstein said. "And no meaningful efforts have been developed to provide real economic development to this region."

This can be described as industries that provide living wages and industries that attract money into the region from outside its boundaries, similar to both the steel and oil industries. Eisenstein mentions this to highlight the lack of economic competition in northwest Indiana.

Couple this thinking with the fact that since 1932 and the election of President Franklin D. Roosevelt, Lake County has become a Democrat Party bastion.

"This has not changed in almost ninety years," Eisenstein said. "There is a single party in northwest Indiana, and it is the Democratic

Party. There have not been any sustained Republican Party challenges to anything countywide."

Are voters at fault more than they would like to believe or admit?

"A free people must be responsible for its actions and decisions," Eisenstein said. "Voters cannot be absolved for failing to pay attention to the deeds, or misdeeds, of those for whom they vote. Personally, I've often been befuddled by the unwillingness to consider voting Republican in northwest Indiana, thereby creating more political competition."

The common stereotype is that the Democratic Party is much more likely to support the "little guy" or the "working class," while the Republican Party is much more interested in supporting "big business" or "the wealthy."

"But here's the thing," Eisenstein said. "The millions of dollars that have been stolen by Democratic elected officials over the decades in Lake County have hurt the little guy and the working class the most, if not solely. Advancing the monetary, political or powered interests of friends and family to the detriment of all the other citizens hurts those who can least afford it. Picking winners and losers in this manner, it is oppressive government, pure and simple."

Essentially, the national perspective of both political parties clouds the decision-making on the local level. Neither political party is monolithic, which is true nationally and even more true locally. That said, it prompts wonderment about the influence of the larger Democratic Party. Where are the voices from the Democratic elite outside of northwest Indiana, those officials who must be aware of what some of their co-party compatriots are doing in this region?

"For example, Robert Pastrick's son became treasurer of the Democratic National Convention when Bill Clinton was in office. At a time when the political power of Pastrick was known outside of northwest Indiana," Eisenstein said. "Alternatively, what about the Republicans? Where has been the effort to convince and persuade voters and citizens? Sure, it is hard, and it might take a while to be successful. But where is the effort? Self-government is hard—where are the elites?"

In effect, we're talking about enduring political corruption that is repeatedly voted for whenever voters elect Democrats in Lake County.

"But who would one vote for? In Gary? In East Chicago? In Lake County government? I am not sure the voters have any real choice, any more than they have in Chicago. I might even suggest that both parties have a gentleman's agreement on how to divide Lake County and they only fight over a small part of it. This *fight* gives some legitimacy to the idea that we have two parties in Lake County."

Lake County treasurer John Petalas points out that the rest of this state knows little to nothing about us, and not coincidentally, we find it difficult to associate ourselves with the rest of the state.

"This is a part of the state that is different from all other parts of Indiana. It always has been," he said. "There was a reason why back in the early part of the last century, our forefathers tried to dis-annex us from the state and name this area Illiana. We are an urban industrial area far away from mainstream Indiana. I think we are greatly misunderstood."

13
Lawyered Up
Defense Attorneys Testify

Many of the most recently indicted public officials in this region were legally represented in court by veteran defense attorney Scott King. In fact, it's somewhat expected to see King's name as the attorney for any high-profile case involving public corruption. This held true again for the region's latest corruption case involving former Lake Station mayor Keith Soderquist, who was found guilty of improperly using funds from his campaign and from the city's food pantry. King, a former mayor of Gary, represented Soderquist, as well as his wife, Deborah Soderquist, who faced similar charges.

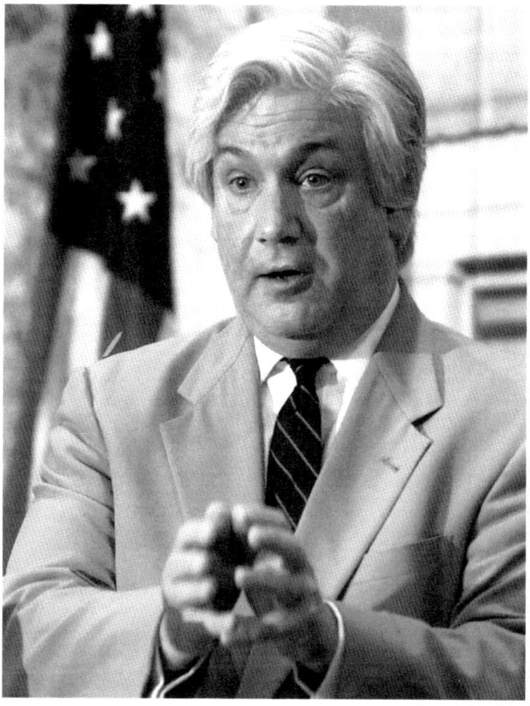

Former Gary mayor Scott King. *Courtesy of Calumet Regional Archives.*

Political insiders suggest following the courtroom trails from defense attorneys such as King to draw parallels between indicted public officials, their legal defenses, their plea deals and their strategies to avoid jail time for their clients. King, for example, is well known for using a "medical condition" defense to successfully receive hearing delays, continuances, special exceptions, reduced sentencing and other benefits for his clients. This strategy could be found in his courtroom defense for former Lake County surveyor George Van Til, former Gary City councilwoman Marilyn Krusas (who died in early 2016) and Deborah Soderquist, whose latest request for a hearing delay was based on health-related issues.

In late September 2016, Deborah Soderquist requested a delay in her sentencing because she had a CT scan scheduled the same day. She also asked the judge for leniency in her sentencing due to several ailments, including treatment for kidney cancer and for medical complications from muscular dystrophy, diabetes and high blood pressure. Through her attorney, she told the judge that incarceration would be detrimental to her health and delay her from getting proper medical treatment. Soderquist asked to serve her twenty-four-month sentence at a halfway house, with the ability to leave for medical treatments.

The judge denied her requests, somewhat surprising anyone who has seen this tactic work successfully in previous cases. As any savvy defense attorney knows, whatever can be done to help a client or reduce a prison sentence will be done in a court of law. It's not always pretty or at all respected by observers, but it's part of the job. Defense attorneys such as King may not be well liked by the general public, but they do earn a certain amount of respect for their resourcefulness and brazenness.

"It's no mystery why these guilty public officials pick Scott King to represent them. He finds any means necessary to help his clients. You and I would pick him, too," said one veteran law enforcement official who's dealt with King on several cases.

Conversely, these attorneys need to scrape the bottom of the barrel for defense tactics when their clients are indicted by federal prosecutors. "The feds never lose a case in court," said Hammond mayor Thomas McDermott, Jr.

There are ninety-four U.S. Attorney's Office districts in the country, including the office for this district, based in Hammond. That office, headed by U.S. attorney David Capp, serves thirty-two Indiana counties and roughly a population of two and a half million Hoosiers. These offices represent the U.S. government in virtually all litigation, criminal

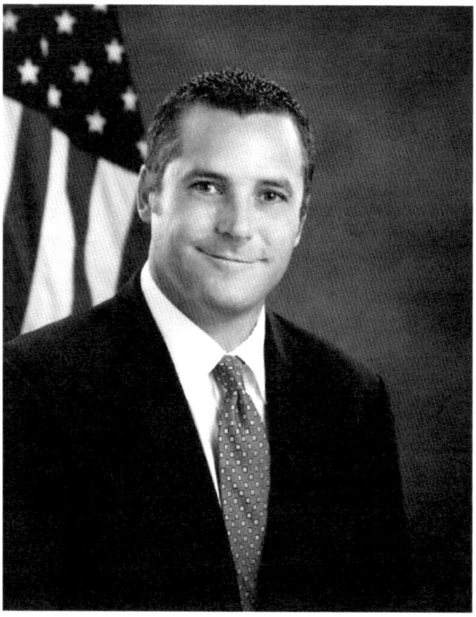

Hammond mayor Thomas McDermott Jr.
Courtesy of Thomas McDermott Jr.

prosecutions, civil lawsuits and actions to collect judgments and restitution on behalf of victims and taxpayers. Criminal cases include gang activity, identity theft, organized crime and, yes, public corruption.

Of all the cases handled by that office, public corruption receives the most public attention and the most dominant front-page headlines. Capp and his staff have taken a zero-tolerance policy against public corruption in this area. That office issues indictments like a doctor issues prescriptions.

"These indictments are part of this office's ongoing public corruption investigation," Capp said in a statement after indicting the Soderquists. "These indictments were the result of an extensive investigative effort by the FBI, IRS and Indiana State Police. This investigative team will continue to investigate allegations of abuse of the public trust."

The public's trust in attorneys, in general, has always been an indictment on the profession. This is especially true in the Calumet region, due to its history with rampant crime and the lawyers who represent criminals in court. Still, many of these attorneys have seen the other side of things when it comes to systemic corruption in local government. Although their courthouse mantra may be "no comment" in public, they, too, have personal opinions about this complex issue, its causes and its remedies.

"This area was born crooked," said veteran defense attorney Thomas Vanes.

Vanes at one time represented Keith Soderquist's stepdaughter, Miranda Brakley, who admitted to embezzling $16,000 from Lake Station City Court while she was employed there as a clerk.

Northwest Indiana, Vanes noted, was one of the last areas in the state to be developed, it had a reputation as a relative wilderness and it gained notoriety as a hideout for criminals, dating back to the nineteenth century.

"The Hammond Packing Company located here because it was not wanted elsewhere. The Aetna Powder Company, then considered a nuisance industry, came here because it was a favorite spot in this desert region," he said, offering only a couple examples of our hardscrabble beginnings. "We live in the financial, social and media orbit of Chicago, but the state line means it has no real obligation to us. Hence, we're the proverbial red-haired stepchild. By the same token, since we're not in the financial, social and media orbit of Indianapolis, it's free to ignore us, as does Chicago."

Vanes equates our geographical location with Camden, New Jersey, describing that troubled city as a "wasting industrial area" just across the border from Philadelphia, Pennsylvania.

"We have the same problems here," Vanes said.

Like many longtime Lake County working professionals, he blames decades of public corruption on the "hammerlock" of Democratic Party rule.

"The local Republican Party is resigned to serving as the Washington Generals to the Democratic Globetrotters," he quipped, referring to the world-famous Harlem Globetrotters and their hapless competitor night in and night out. "And with the same modus operandi—create the appearance of competition, try not to get in the way, and collect a paycheck just the same. The Washington Generals lost over ten thousand games in that fashion."

"When you don't have to compete for votes in a general election, then government officials are selected by the byzantine politics of primary elections. And the result is often a kakistocracy, a government run by the most unqualified or least principled citizens," Vanes said.

Vanes cites the example of former East Chicago police chief Stephen "Bob" Stiglich, who died in 2005 at age seventy. During his tenure as East Chicago's top law enforcement officer, the city's parks department superintendent was murdered execution-style, and a prominent East Chicago attorney was murdered at a political fundraiser, with ballistic evidence tampered with while in police custody. Both cases were never solved, Vanes said.

"But voters here went on to elect Stiglich as Lake County sheriff, Lake County auditor, and he also became chairman of the Democratic Party. Only in Lake County," Vanes said. "Why? The large number of people here dependent upon the largesse of those like him for jobs, election favors and the like. Plus, an electorate that is more parochial than normal, with little concern for much beyond our borders or much beyond today and tomorrow. As the writer Solzhenitsyn observed, the line separating good from evil is not

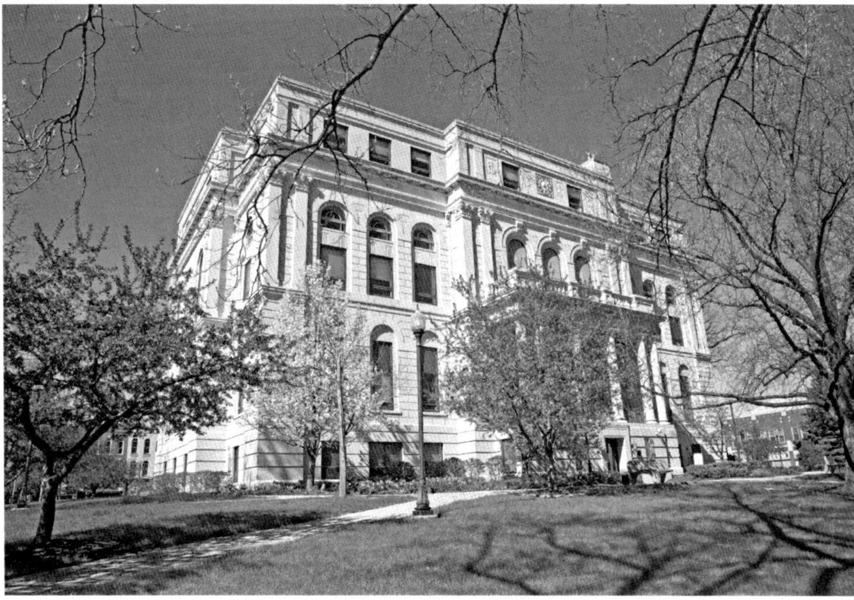

Porter County Courthouse, Valparaiso, Indiana. *Courtesy of Joey Lax-Salinas.*

a line separating nations or races or parties. It is a line cutting through each and every human heart. And it's a thin line, too."

John H. Davis, a veteran attorney from Merrillville, said the fact that Lake County's infamous reputation exists only increases the amount of corruption in this region.

"The reputation itself is the moving force for corruption," Davis said. "Reputation influences many who may not have a penchant for corruption to be motivated by the ease that facilitates corruption, as well as the perceived rewards of such corruption."

"Additionally, the concentration of economics held in the hands of a few also motivates many individuals who feel left out in the participation of the scarce financial opportunities that flow into the region," Davis said. "The few hands which are able to take charge of the scarce financial opportunities here manipulate, many times illegally, the scarce financial opportunities in fear of being one of the many who have no chance to wield this control."

Davis disagrees that it's simply a problem of one-party rule for so long.

"I don't think it's something darker and deeper, but I believe it is simply a matter of nepotism and cronyism," he said. "In this type of environment, it is difficult for one who is not related or known to the power structure to be accepted, or to enter that small select group. In this way, it may be like a caste system."

"It appears that the voters and citizens in this region tend to be somewhat slothful in their exercise of the electoral process, thus they unfortunately get what they deserve," Davis noted. "Not to say that this constitutes all of the voters and citizens of this region."

Davis, who was born and raised in New York City, understands that corruption is a societal problem that takes decades to implant in any area.

"Corruption is infectious, and it takes a while to become a permanent or insidious part of a region," he said. "Public corruption is continuing to take place in the present day, and it's fueled by the increasing attitude that the means justify the end. That is, corruption is not thought of by many to be morally wrong."

"In fact, the thought of reputation as the means in which a good person lives their life is no longer considered to be the manner in which one should live their lives. This attitude comes from individuals holding high positions in corporate America, the political arena, and thus influences all individuals—young and old—to take the position that it is not a taint on one's character to commit illegal and immoral acts," Davis said.

What can or should be done to remedy these social ills?

"I believe increased transparency regarding spending by any entity of public funds will help address this chronic disease," Davis replied. "This would entail enacting policies and laws that must be followed when spending public funds. This would include impartial review committees mandated to oversee accounting and procedural practices relating to all agencies and entities receiving public funds."

Too many politicians initially start out with high ideals and honest desires to serve the public, he believes. Unfortunately, this quickly changes when a politician seeks to make beneficial or needed changes in society, yet these measures require fellow politicians to endorse or support their projects.

"Often the support comes with strings attached, and those strings are corrupt, thus those politicians succumb to corruption," Davis said.

Vanes had a more comical response to what's needed to combat public corruption in Lake County.

"The U.S. Marines? Batman?" he joked.

14
Behind Bars
Firsthand Accounts from Sentenced Pols

A handful of former northwest Indiana officials who have been convicted for public corruption—and have served time in prison for their crimes—agreed to speak with me for this book. They did so, however, under the agreement of anonymity to protect themselves from violating their probation and to avoid getting hassled again by federal authorities. "That's the last thing I need in my life since finally being released from prison," said one former public officeholder who spent time behind bars.

For starters, each of these former elected officials took offense to my initial subtitle for this book, "Tall Tales and Short Sentences." "Short sentence?" asked one incredulous public official. "I have a *lifetime* sentence, and it started in the court of public opinion ever since I got indicted."

These sources claimed they were released from prison with little or no money to their names, no savings of any kind and no job opportunities that come remotely close to their former positions and income levels. They also have a new reputation to live down, a new tainted legacy and the realization that the feds will always have their eyes on them. "No matter what we do or where we go, we feel we're still being followed," said one source who insisted on a face-to-face meeting—as opposed to a phone call, which could be recorded.

Formally, these men served probation for either a few months or a few years. But informally, they feel they're on probation until they're dead. One official who served time in a federal correctional facility said he still gets treated strangely during casual exchanges in public. "People literally don't stand as close to me as they used to," he said. "It's done on a very subconscious level. They don't even realize they're doing it. But I do."

The political insiders said there are two kinds of public corruption: public servants who slowly "slide into" corruption by condoning or pursuing shady deeds that border on criminal acts and public servants who have premeditated intentions of criminal activity before getting elected or appointed into office. Nonetheless, once incarcerated, they're just another inmate, dealing with their time behind bars.

"Some do it with anger or religion, and others do it with delusions of innocence," one former inmate said from firsthand experience. "Whatever gets you through each night."

What's a typical day in a federal correctional facility?

"It's exactly the same as the day before, and exactly as the day after," replied one source.

These former inmates couldn't help but notice they served time in prison with brazen criminals who committed much harsher crimes, including manslaughter and multimillion-dollar Ponzi schemes. Yet they were also incarcerated with other former public servants convicted of tax evasion, sentenced to what equated to a slap on the wrist from the U.S. justice system.

"In Lake County, you're a fool if you plead not guilty and go to trial," one former public official told me. "What jury would find any of us innocent, considering our county's reputation? During my career, not a single elected or appointed public official in Lake County has ever been found not guilty. Come on, you can't say that the feds are *that* good or the public officials are *that* bad."

Lake County is well known for its public corruption, but it should also be well known for federal authorities who make a career by targeting politicians in this region, one informant told me.

"It's like fishing in a barrel," he said. "They absolutely believe that every politician in the Lake County government center is a crook, yet they haven't been indicted."

Another source said, "The feds specialize in what they do, so they're going to find something on pretty much anyone they investigate. Don't be fooled. The feds play a huge role in why this seems to happen in Lake County more than in other counties."

The feds, they say, have seemingly bottomless resources, unlimited legal research capabilities and governmental legalities in their back pocket.

"Plus, they turn everything into a federal case, literally, by finding the proper legal criteria to charge someone, whether it's through wiretapping, mail fraud or whatever," explained one source. "Federal indictments are very carefully crafted."

Another politician concluded, "It's like gambling at a casino. The house always wins."

15
What Can or Should Be Done?

What can be done about northwest Indiana's and, more specifically, Lake County's political culture, which breeds so much public corruption? Are the latest convictions the death knell for corruption? Or is our history our destiny?

"How do you change this culture?" asked Marie Eisenstein.

"For starters, we need to quit exaggerating a problem that exists all over America," said Lake County treasurer John Petalas. "We need to quit making it unique to Lake County, because it isn't. We need to accentuate the positive in Lake County. We need developers and out-of-state people curious about the region to read the good things that are a part of this region."

"Public corruption has become a big deal in everyone's vocabulary because local media has made it a big deal," Petalas said. "There are over three hundred elected and appointed officials in this county. They are not all crooks. In fact, 99 percent of them are good honest people who do their jobs and go home at the end of the day. But the news media makes the remaining 1 percent make the 99 percent look bad."

Petalas offered an idea to help kick start this new public image campaign.

"How about a newspaper column titled, 'Yours in public service,' that would showcase elected and appointed officials at least once a month who work their ass off to serve the taxpayer?" he suggested. "Law enforcement will do the rest."

Jim Flannery, former executive director of the Northwest Indiana Quality of Life Council, said, "As long as there is no firm commitment

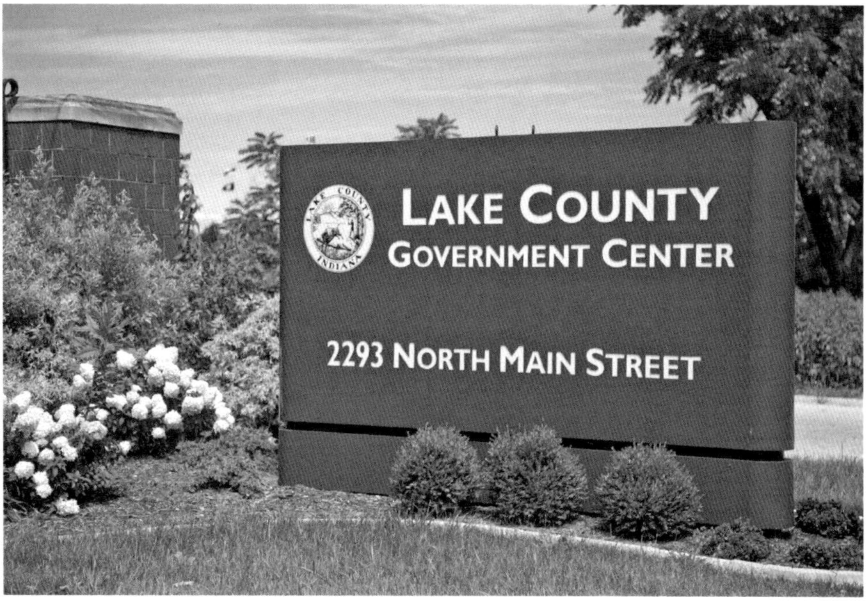

Lake County Government Complex, Crown Point, Indiana. *Courtesy of Joey Lax-Salinas.*

to ethics in government and appropriate checks and balances, coupled with public watchdog organizations to call out corruption, I feel it will continue."

Hammond mayor Thomas McDermott Jr. believes we should strive to reduce the number of Lake County elected officials—and with it, competing agendas—through some type of "Uni-Gov" proposal.

"This would increase the focus on the remaining elected officials to coordinate regionalism and coordination between the many municipalities in Lake County," he said. "If we want to think regionally, we need to set up our government in northwest Indiana like they did in Marion County, Indiana, in the 1970s. This concept centralized power into a single, high profile mayor and a single, high profile city-county council."

"As Lake County grew and its population climbed, it became exponentially harder for the county to get on the same page regionally. The number of elected officials grew exponentially as well, making it harder for the average voter to keep track of it all."

Along with many other elected officials and concerned residents, McDermott is convinced that a stronger media presence is needed, one that focuses exclusively on northwest Indiana, not the Chicagoland area.

"The fact that Lake County relies only upon two newspapers and three news radio stations to educate the public on what is happening is surely part of the problem with regard to the uneducated voters," McDermott said. "If we had a viable TV station, or stations, focusing solely on Lake County, the unethical elected officials would have more to worry about as far as potentially being exposed for their wrongdoings. An educated and informed voter is the best tool for fighting against corruption in government, that's for sure."

Dan Blankenship, a Republican who serves as Cedar Creek Township Board president, agrees with McDermott, likely an uncommon agreement between two public servants with diametrically opposed political views.

"I definitely think if we had a viable television station here in northwest Indiana, it would play a huge role in getting elected officials to pay attention to what they're doing and how they're doing it," Blankenship said. "I don't think our elected officials fear the local newspapers at all."

"If we had a major television station that people watched every night, things might be slightly different," he added. "I sometimes wonder if people think that they even have to watch out for their local officials and what they're doing. It is really hard to attend local meetings and listen to what's being discussed. Most of us definitely don't have time to investigate our elected officials."

Blankenship suggests, "More online oversight that the average Joe can look up. By making it easier for us to see the flow of money and authority, you let the public know if things seem right or if there's questions to be asked. I truly think the advancement of communications through computers has helped uncover a lot of the shenanigans."

Lake County historian Bruce Woods points to the chronic problem of territorialism and parochialism throughout this multi-county region.

"County lines, city lines, even township lines seem to become barriers for cooperation and working for the common good," he said. "Just as with Gary, so many people feel Gary's problems are not our problems. They could not be more wrong."

Eisenstein said possible solutions may go back to her earlier assertions regarding the dominance of one political party.

"There are many things that kept one-party rule going, even post–World War II," she said. "The ability to dispense the rewards from a federal program certainly helped. So does a reliance on vote fraud. But think about what has happened in the last ten to fifteen years with property tax reform in Indiana? Out of ninety-nine counties in Indiana, there were only two

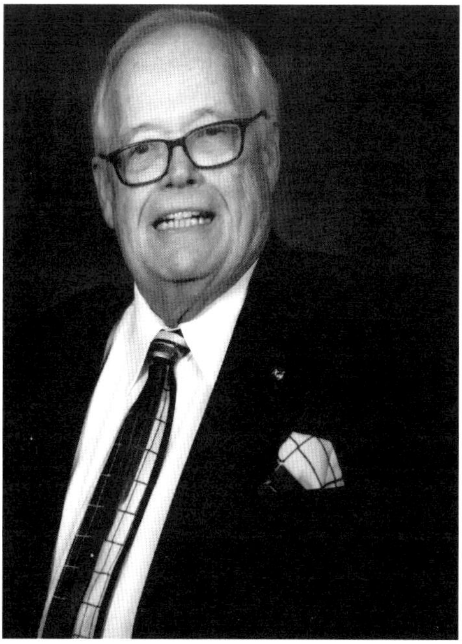

Lake County Historical Society president Bruce Woods. *Courtesy of Bruce Woods.*

counties that could not live on the 1-2-3 model of tax caps. Lake County was one of those. Northwest Indiana has, and historically had, an impressive industrial tax base. That tax base poured millions upon millions of dollars into local city treasuries."

For decades, these localities were able to keep property taxes artificially low for homeowners.

"This enabled one-party rule to attract the middle-class homeowner vote, in addition to the traditional immigrant vote," Eisenstein said. "When the Indiana Supreme Court ruled that tax reform must be accomplished, the tax revenue from industry decreased. Maybe this is the beginning of the demise for the one-party and party machine rule in northwest Indiana. Maybe."

Thomas Frank, an outspoken environmental activist from East Chicago, tends to lean toward an abstract understanding of the word "corruption."

"For the past decade I've tended to associate corruption with organized plausible deniability, an intentional separation between agency and a desired effect as recording in the public record," he explained. "It appears to me that our political economy trains-up groups and individuals to operate in this space of plausible deniability. I'm not certain corruption is any more rampant here than anywhere else. We are a region of conflicting narratives under the brute force of industrial capitalism."

"Good Government" narratives are owned by those industrial forces to keep political unrest in line, he noted.

"It is mostly out of this framing that so-called public corruption has been used," Frank said. "Our politics is so fractured and, even when I mettle with it, I add to the fracturing. Part of the problem is the earnestness of ignorance. My own included. What I mean by this is that even naïve people recognize their intentions, and those intentions are always good. In a complex, fractured region, people naturally focus on their good intentions and neglect their effect."

The word *ethics* comes up repeatedly when exploring possible solutions to corruption, but critics question its effectiveness in a region notorious for criminal activities within local government.

"Ethics training and a pledge to be ethical isn't going to solve anything," said Kim Krull. "In fact I believe it only gives a false sense of 'everything's OK now.'"

Krull reiterated her recommendation of a compliance officer and a strong two-party system of government at the county level, which would provide the proper checks and balances.

"Hiring qualified people to run departments instead of electing them would help also," she added. "We should hire the best qualified county recorder, auditor, assessor, treasurer, and so on, and have fewer elected positions."

Most everyone agrees that U.S. attorney David Capp and his office of federal prosecutors have done a stellar job, targeting their efforts on a problem that has made this region a punchline for far too long.

"I am not sure there is anything that can be done in any reasonable time frame," Eisenstein said, echoing the skepticism of tens of thousands of region residents. "That's being as honest as anyone can be. The reason I say this is that it appears as if no level of prosecution makes a dent in the ongoing nature of corruption in Lake County, Indiana."

Petalas countered by noting, "The problem still exists, but even federal law enforcement officers will tell you it's not as bad as it once was. Public corruption will never go away. Neither will murder, burglary, armed robbery or any other criminal classification."

Petalas has a valid point. So did this unheeded advice from a *Northwest Indiana Sentinel* newspaper story in 1964.

"Lake County voters must become better informed on the backgrounds and qualifications of candidates for public office, and to show more responsibility than they have in the past in the selection of their nominees. If voters blanch at seeing pictures and reading stories of more public corruption scandals, they must remember it was their votes that put officials responsible for those things in office."

Epilogue

An Author's Epiphany

While conducting countless interviews and research projects for this book, I soon realized that this topic is a never-ending endeavor in northwest Indiana. Each time I thought that every corrupt or convicted politician from this region was noted somewhere within these pages, I discovered yet another disgraced public officeholder who, ahem, *deserves* a mention of some kind.

My research attempts felt like pulling weeds in a long-neglected garden of shame and secrecy. New weeds from seedy names kept sprouting up in unexpected places. And deep-rooted stories, some from decades ago, kept leading to even deeper subplots, buried far below the surface of public knowledge.

Some of them I unearthed for this book; others I stopped pulling up when I realized their roots were entangled in lies, rumors or misinformation. Some sources coughed up names strictly for historical accuracy. Others did so because they had an axe to grind. My response was the same to everyone: I was allowed only a certain number of words, pages and images for this book, so I focused on an opinionated overview of the topic rather than writing exclusively about a few of the more infamous names, scandals and court trials over the past century.

I learned so much about the art and science of public corruption while sorting through innumerable old documents, online stories and dusty interviews from a laundry list of sources. However, I also learned that an entire book series could be written on this exhaustive subject. I'll leave that to another author with more pages at his or her disposal. Like everything in my time-stamped life, this book was written on a deadline that didn't budge.

Looking back, I'm sure I neglected to note certain names or specific corruption-related crimes, so please accept my apologies in advance. However, as I'm writing this, I'm convinced that elected officials somewhere in northwest Indiana are committing some kind of crime at taxpayers' expense. Yes, possibly at this very moment, regardless of when you read this sentence. Of course the tight-lipped U.S. Attorney's Office in Hammond has no comment regarding ongoing public corruption investigations.

However, when I posed this likely scenario to a federal prosecutor who has worked extensively on public corruption cases in this region, he could only smile. Off the record, he told me that my suspicions are likely correct, though no names were uttered. It's hard to believe after all these decades, all these indictments and all these convictions that a public official would dare commit a crime of any kind, even stealing a handful of paperclips.

Then again, it's Lake County, Indiana. Furthermore, it's not that hard to believe when you consider the human dynamics at work, the same universal dynamics that existed a century ago, corrupting so many others after they were elected into public office. Those damning attributes won't go away:

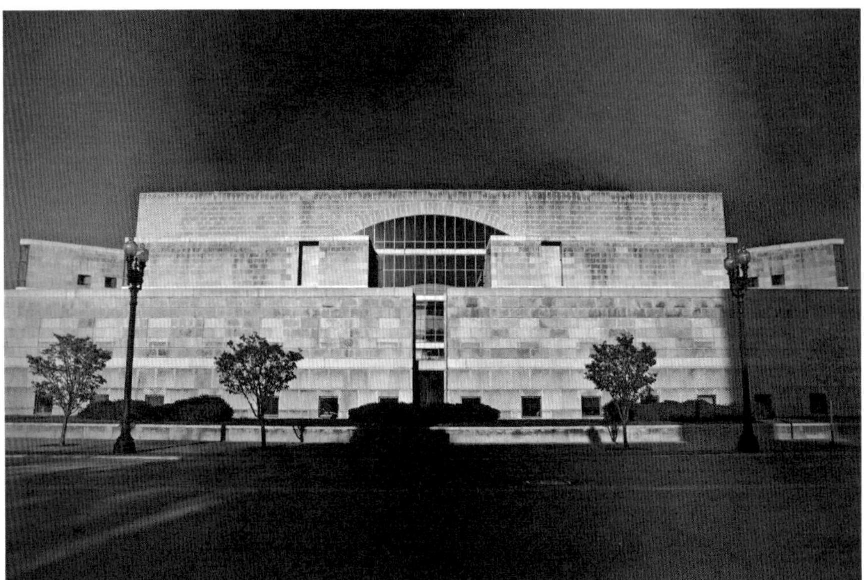

U.S. District Court Federal Courthouse, Hammond, Indiana, at night. *Courtesy of Joey Lax-Salinas.*

greed, ego, arrogance, the lust for power, disillusioned entitlement and, of course, a timeless feeling of invincibility.

By the time you're reading this last paragraph, it's likely that federal prosecutors have indicted, if not convicted and sentenced, yet another public official who has disgraced his or her family, added to the infamy of this region and, probably, shifted blame to someone or something else. This, too, is the *region* way.

Glossary

anonymous shell companies: companies that do little or no actual business. Instead, they often exist and function entirely on paper, opening bank accounts and owning assets without ever revealing the name of the true person benefiting from its conduct, whether legal or illicit.

backroom deals: a place where powerful or influential people, especially politicians, meet to plan secretly and exercise control in an indirect manner.

bootleggers: criminals who made or sold alcohol illegally, typically during Prohibition.

bribes: money or favors given or promised in order to influence the judgment or conduct of a person in a position of trust.

coffers: money available for spending on various expenditures.

collusion: secret agreement or cooperation especially for an illegal or deceitful purpose.

conspiracy: a secret plan made by two or more people to do something harmful or illegal.

extortion: the crime of obtaining money from someone through use of force or threats.

G-men: a special agent of the U.S. Federal Bureau of Investigation (FBI).

graft: the acquisition of money, gain or advantage by dishonest, unfair or illegal means, especially through the abuse of one's position or influence in politics or business.

grand jury: a group of people who look at evidence against someone accused of a crime in order to decide if there should be a trial.

hush money: money paid so that someone will keep information secret.

indictment: a formal written statement framed by a prosecuting authority and found by a jury (as a grand jury) charging a person with an offense.

kickback: money given to someone in return for providing help in a secret and dishonest business deal.

mail fraud: a crime in which the perpetrator develops a scheme using mailings to swindle another out of money or property. This crime specifically requires the intent to defraud and is a federal offense governed by section 1341 of title 18 of the U.S. Code. The mail fraud statute was first enacted in 1872 to prohibit illicit mailings with the U.S. Postal Service (formerly the U.S. Post Office) for the purpose of executing a fraudulent scheme.

malfeasance: the performance by a public official of an act that is legally unjustified, harmful or contrary to law; wrongdoing (used especially of an act in violation of a public trust).

money grabs: an undignified or unprincipled acquisition of a large sum of money with little effort.

money laundering: criminally hiding or disguising the source of illegal money by converting it to funds that appear legitimate.

nepotism: the unfair practice by a powerful person of giving jobs or other professional favors to family members or relatives.

organized crime: a group of professional criminals who work together as part of a powerful and secret organization.

payoffs: money, valuables or favors given to someone for doing something illegal or dishonest.

pol: abbreviation for politician.

political powerbroker: a person who influences people to vote toward a particular client (e.g., elected official or referendum) in exchange for political and financial benefits. Powerbrokers can also negotiate deals with other powerbrokers to meet their aims.

protection money: a sum of money paid to a gang leader or criminal that will ensure a business is safe from attack by other gangs or criminals operating in the area. Payment is usually made due to threats about nonpayment against the business owner.

public corruption: a breach of public trust and/or abuse of position by federal, state or local officials and their private sector accomplices.

racketeering: making money through illegal activities.

scandal: an occurrence outraging people due to behavior that is considered morally or legally wrong.

scapegoat: a person who is unfairly blamed for something that others have done.

sting operation: in law enforcement, a deceptive operation designed to catch a person or organization committing a crime.

stool pigeon: a criminal who gives the police information about other criminals.

straw man: a weak or imaginary argument or opponent that is set up to be easily defeated.

shakedown: the act of taking something (such as money) from someone by using threats or deception.

suspicious funds: money acquired illegally that has been converted to apparently legitimate funds (see "money laundering").

tax evasion: a willful and especially criminal attempt to avoid the imposition or payment of a tax.

tax violations: a taxpayer's intent to defraud the government by not paying taxes that he or she knows are lawfully due.

vice syndicate: a group of people involved in organized crime.

vituperation: harsh and angry criticism.

WCC: Women's Citizens Committee, formed in Gary in the 1950s to clean up the city's criminal element.

wiretapping: placing a device on someone's phone to secretly listen to calls.

Bibliography

Books

Davich, Jerry. *Lost Gary, Indiana*. Charleston, SC: The History Press, 2015.
Lane, James B. *City of the Century*. Bloomington: Indiana University Press, 1978.
Svengalis, Kendall. *Gary, Indiana: A Centennial Celebration*. North Stonington, CT: Duneland Press, 2006.

Material Sources

Calumet Regional Archives, Indiana University Northwest.
East Chicago Public Library
Gary Public Library
Hammond Public Library
Lake Station City Hall
Lake Station Public Library

NEWSPAPERS

Chicago Tribune
(*Crown Point, IN*) *Post Tribune*
(*Munster, IN*) *Times*
Newsweek. "Cities: Gary Cleanup." May 21, 1949.
Northwest Indiana Sentinel

REPORTS

Northwest Indiana Crime Commission Report, August 1962.
Northwest Indiana Crime Commission Report, October 1963.

Index

F

G

H

I

J

K

L

M

N

O

P

Q

R

S

T

V

W

Z

About the Photographer

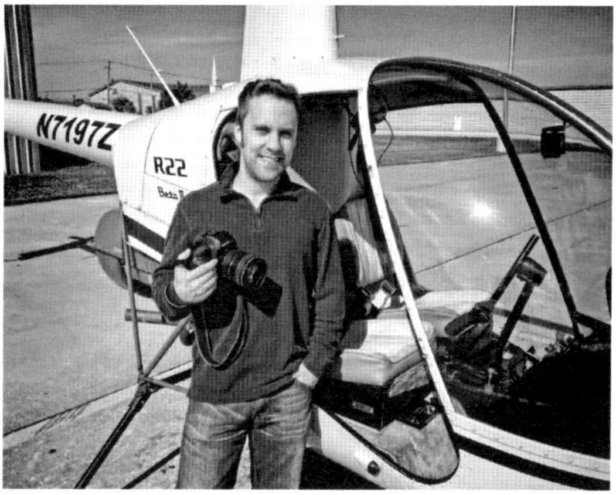

Joey Lax-Salinas. *Courtesy of Joey Lax-Salinas.*

Joey Lax-Salinas is a traveling photographer and video producer as well as a lifelong resident of northwest Indiana. Originally from Hammond, Indiana, Joey has collected and archived thousands of market-ready photos of northwest Indiana covering every city and town in a six-county region. Joey's photos are located at www.JoeyLaxSalinas.com and are available for purchase as prints or can be licensed for commercial use.

About the Author

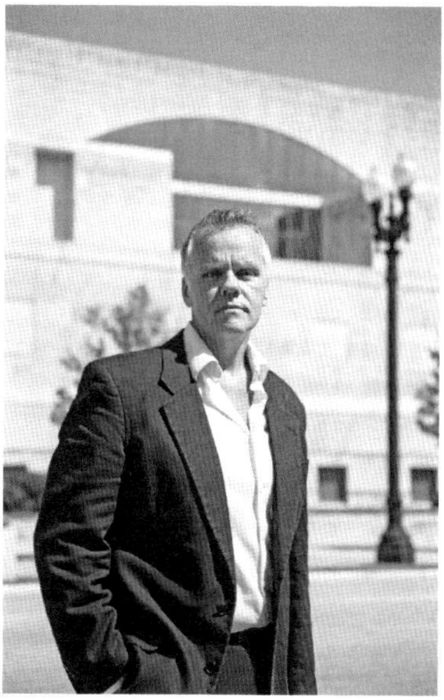

Jerry Davich. *Courtesy of Joey Lax-Salinas.*

Jerry Davich was born and raised in Lake County, Indiana, where he learned the hardscrabble reality of political corruption in the Calumet region.

Jerry's journalism career began in 1995 as a political cartoonist for the *Times* newspaper before becoming a newspaper reporter and, in 2006, metro columnist for the *Post-Tribune* newspaper/Chicago Tribune Media.

He has always shined a light on society's darkest corners and offered a voice to the voiceless while writing about myriad issues, events and people in northwest Indiana and beyond.

Jerry has earned more than forty-five state or national awards from various journalism organizations for his work, including countless columns on public corruption and its ripples throughout northwest Indiana.

He also is author of the books *Connections: Everyone Happens for a Reason* and *Lost Gary, Indiana*.

Jerry lives in Valparaiso with his wife, Karen, and he never leaves home without his pen, notebook and curiosity.

Visit us at
www.historypress.net

This title is also available as an e-book